Types *Best Forgotten*

A

COLLECTION

OF

OBSERVATIONS

ON

Types *Best Forgotten*

BY

VARIOUS

PEOPLE

UNCHARITABLY

DISPOSED

TO

ALL SORTS

OF

DIFFERENT THINGS

A typeface
is an
alphabet
in a
straightjacket.

Alan Fletcher is one of those designers who never seems to have been as unknown as most of the rest of us. It was Alan Fletcher; then Fletcher, Forbes & Gill; then Crosby, Fletcher, Forbes; and then Pentagram, where he seemed to have grown roots. And now he has come full circle, back to Alan Fletcher.

And he has achieved it all with the handicap of having gone to the same school as both Sebastian Carter and the editor. What could he not have done had he had a proper education!

All Typefaces Drawn Since Film

and offset printing became the norm that appear to re-invent an earlier age. Soft serifs and exaggerated angles – art nouveau, jazz age, arts & crafts movement – the catalogues are full of them. And not one with any wit.

All the classic reportary faces redrawn with bloated lowercase x heights and ten or more added weights and widths.

Typefaces altered in detail to avoid some copyright restriction or other.

Pet dislikes: Palatino for its clever mock tablet inscription-like seriousness. Melior, just downright nasty – and having had to use it once.

And so on – don't touch anything from ITC – well, with the possible exception of their Baskerville – which they bought in, and didn't get around to pushing up the x height and adding 50 different weights, widths etc. Their Caslon is indescribably vulgar – and, while I'm at it, what they did with Franklin Gothic was completely unnecessary! The weights, the numbers – yuk!

I can't really say I'm too keen on any of Mr Zapf's contributions to the art of type design.

One's tastes change of course. Once I would have campaigned for Haas' drawing of Aksidenz Grotesk over Univers. Now I rather like Univers, and of course there is nothing wrong with Helvetica anyway. It took me some years to appreciate Gill's typefaces. Now I won't hear any criticism. He was a genius.

DENNIS BAILEY

abcdefghijklmnopqrstuvwxyz
ABCDEFGHIJKLMNOPQRSTUVWXYZ
1234567890 .,:;''«»ß&!?

abcdefghijklmnopqrstuvwxyz
ABCDEFGHIJKLMNOPQRSTUVWXYZ
1234567890 .,:;''«»ß&!?

abcdefghijklmnopqrstuvwxyz
ABCDEFGHIJKLMNOPQRSTUVWXYZ
1234567890 .,:;''«»ß&!?

Those who have known Dennis over the more than thirty years that he has been making silk purses of what have often been the sow's ears of numerous periodicals are perhaps the only ones who know how much he has influenced the way magazines look in Britain today. It is also astonishing to many of us how he ever manages to get these jobs done when he can easily spend a day considering the best way to assemble the letters that he needs to make three words. It is not astonishing, though, that he was elected a Royal Designer for Industry.

Anything

designed since Palatino.

COLIN COHEN

abcdefghijklmnopqrstuvwxyz
ABCDEFGHIJKLMNOPQRSTUVWXYZ
1234567890 .,:;''«»ß&!?

abcdefghijklmnopqrstuvwxyz
ABCDEFGHIJKLMNOPQRSTUVWXYZ
1234567890 .,:;''«»ß&!?

abcdefghijklmnopqrstuvwxyz
ABCDEFGHIJKLMNOPQRSTUVWXYZ

If you need to know something about the graphic industry, there are conventional ways of solving the problem. You can go to libraries. You can subscribe to trade magazines. You can visit shows. You can do all of these things. But if you would rather spend time on the beach you need do none of these things. You just ask Colin Cohen.

All Semi-Bolds

except for Meridian

MATTHEW CARTER

abcdefghijklmnopqrstuvwxyz
ABCDEFGHIJKLMNOPQRSTUVWXYZ
1234567890 .,:;"«»ß&!?

Matthew Carter inherited from his father Harry a taste for typographical history and a talent for type-cutting and type design. After working freelance in London during the swinging sixties, having learnt punchcutting in Harlem at Enschedeen en Zonen, he was hired by Mergenthaler Linotype in Brooklyn to draw types. Later he created the firm of Bitstream in Cambridge, Mass. with Mike Parker. Best known for his design of Galliard, he is a lanky, lucid and influential figure upon the typographical scene to which he contributes a great deal in design and dogma.
J D

All Typefaces

For some time type has paralysed the faces of writing. Their mummified bodies are laid out in the catalogues of the typefounders. A stop of 500 years in the development of text scripts is long enough to make one look upon formal writing as static. Against a continuous tradition of 5000 years, however, the interruption has been merely incidental.

The techniques of punch cutting, striking matrices and casting type made the standstill unavoidable, but this serious disadvantage was unnecessarily upgraded to be a typographic virtue. Whereas the obstructing techniques are forgotten, the opportunistic ideal of petrified writing survives. From a traditional typographic point of view type design is drifting. But it is only the provisional standard that has fallen away. Everybody can now again take his own responsibility for his own writing just as everybody had to do during past millennia, and just as we have always accepted our responsibility for our own language.

We are only recently beginning to see the new opportunities for type design. In one regard the numerous typefaces in the typefounders' catalogues are all the same: all text scripts have been tailored for the average job. They might have met this condition fairly, but I do not know if this is so, because I am a designer. Designers never get average jobs to do. They are only engaged for special tasks surpassing the printer's routine.

GERRIT NOORDZIJ

abcdefghijklmnopqrstuvwxyz
ABCDEFGHIJKLMNOPQRSTUVWXYZ
1234567890 1234567890 .,:;''«»ß&!?

abcdefghijklmnopqrstuvwxyz
ABCDEFGHIJKLMNOPQRSTUVWXYZ
1234567890 1234567890 .,:;''«»ß&!?

It is risky to say anything about this man. His thoughts are always original. His
design is always his own. His teaching has been exceptional, and his students are
now beginning to overrun Europe, and perhaps the best thing they have learned
from him is never to think in clichés.
But it is wise to have a place near the door if you have been silly enough to make
a foolish or provocative statement in his hearing.
Otherwise you may never hear the last of it.

All Unauthorised Copies

If anybody wants to know which typefaces I do not like there is a simple answer. I must confess that they are all the bad and unauthorized copies of the creative work of other designers whose very faults diminish the original design. Other people will judge the face and the designer by what they see, little knowing that the faults are in the copy and not in the original.

This complaint is separate from the one I am also entitled to make, that many firms are making money from selling these copies. Not a nickel is shared with the original designer.

HERMANN ZAPF

CALAMINE
CARNATION
GERANIUM
GILB
MALLIOR
MULLION
TEMPORA
etc.

Hermann is easily the best known of contemporary type designers. His long association with the Stempel foundry must have made significant differences to how large a suitcase was needed to carry money to the bank of the parent company, Linotype AG. Palatino, Optima and Melior have all been best sellers, and probably all share two other unique distinctions. They all appeared, in turn, as the typeface most used on the letterhead of a great many leading design groups. And, except for Helvetica, they may be the most often copied faces of modern times. In the best known examples the imitation is deliberate. Most foundries, hampered in the sales of hardware because they couldn't license these faces, came out with similar – but often mechanical looking – copies. But another aspect has been that these three and also Aldus are each echoed again and again in the typefaces designed at art schools all over the world. More than once I have listened to a young designer explain the philosophy behind his new design, sometimes in Hermann's hearing, entirely unaware that, perhaps subliminally, what he has made has already been better made with one of these four faces.

Alphabet Soup

In your list of letters we hope never to see again I should like to add one; namely the wishy-washy ubiquitous sans serif in alphabet soup.

ERIC BLEGVAD

Erik Blegvad, a devoted disciple of the great tradition of Danish illustrators like Ib Andersen, arrived in Paris after the war equipped with a French vocabulary consisting of little more than, 'Oui, je parle français courament'. But in no time at all he was drawing for Elle, and for other publishers, and embarking on a long career of book illustration. It was in Paris that he met Lenore, and in due course they returned to her American home where he broke into both the US magazine world and the world of childrens' book publishing, together with many other friends, like Nils Mons Bodecker. In addition to this his annual calendar for Womans Day has become a collector's item, especially since the year that it included a view from the editor's balcony in Seattle.

Bored by Bembo

In the days when they kept such records – and perhaps they still do – I could never understand why Bembo, together with Times, was the face that appeared most frequently in the annual *50 Best Books.* A surfeit of Bembo made me long for the vigorous toughies like Bell and Walbaum or even the plain but honest Imprint.

Its inherent gentility brought out the vulgarian in me and made me want to behave like a typographical hooligan – all sans and no spacing.

Printed letterpress from metal type it was tolerable but uninspiring. When it was translated into film for offset insufficient allowance was made for the lack of ink squeeze and its weaknesses became more evident – the over-careful curves and that infuriatingly soggy tail on the R. It has pulled itself together a bit in digital form but I would still rather not use it.

In the hands of graphic designers it has moved out of bookwork onto emasculated signs and shop fronts. The sooner it is put back into the type cases where the private press boys can do something with it the better.

JOHN MILES

abcdefghijklmnopqrstuvwxyz
ABCDEFGHIJKLMNOPQRSTUVWXYZ
1234567890 .,:;''«»ß&!?

abcdefghijklmnopqrstuvwxyz
ABCDEFGHIJKLMNOPQRSTUVWXYZ
1234567890 .,:;''«»ß&!?

One of the adages learned by graphic design students in their foundation course is
'The least said about John Miles the better.' But lost in the mists of time is the
origin of the saying. Some people think that it is because it is unwise to adopt a
rôle model you cannot hope to emulate.
I can now reveal that to be able to concentrate on doing good work when you are
inexorably and irrevocably tied by an umbilical cord to a large hole in the ground
in Suffolk is something that only John Miles can manage. Here, in relative safety at
weekends, he can grow vegetables and paint without having to duck every time the
low flying aircraft that buzz Snape and the whole Aldeburgh area pass overhead.

Brush Script

The brush was invented long before moveable type and it no doubt produced some beautiful letter forms. But if it was the intention of Robert E Smith to create a beautiful script letter form in moveable type he did not succeed.

Those wonderful printers and lettercutters who advanced the arts and the age of civilisation with their wonderful works must have had an extra pour or two of Glenlivet the day ATF introduced Brush Script to the trade (God surely must allow such lovely refreshments, in moderation of course).

I always believed that those people who set 'all cap' headlines in Brush Script had a wonderful sense of humour. Surely they only wanted to show Mr Smith what a terrible typeface he had created.

Of course, if Robert E Smith lived today, he might point to what has happened to the typographic art as a result of the desktop publishing revolution, and demand an apology from me.

Perhaps a wee bit of Glenlivet would temper his position.

DON HASE

ABCDEFGHIJKLMNOP2RS
abcdefghijklmnopqrstuvwxyz$$123456

Don Hase can't have been more than sixteen or so when he was first thrown into the world of typesetting, and before long he was lucky enough to come into the orbit of the great Allan Friedman. Al in turn was busy building the capital base that finally launched Alphatype. He designed, assembled and marketed the first large selling headline photosetter, the Filmotype.

Don has probably been responsible for making more film fonts than anybody before or after him. Even in the early sixties he had made hundreds at a time when most people didn't even know what a film font was.

By now, when he has moved on to other activities nearer the 'leading edge' than boring old type, nobody would be able to make a count.

Cheltenham

My apprenticeship as a compositor began more than forty years ago in a London caseroom plentifully stocked with Cheltenham; a face I quickly came to dislike. I had to set stickfuls of the founts mainly for displayed material. It is a design irredeemably lacking in charm or comeliness of any kind. Clumpy serifs and poor proportions rapidly conjure a nightmarish typographic vision. Originally created by Bertram Goodhue in 1896 for Ingalls Kimball of the Cheltenham Press in New York, Cheltenham remained exclusive to that enterprise until the early years of the twentieth century when developed for the trade into an extensive family by the American Type Founders Company and by the Mergenthaler Linotype Company, principally through the initial efforts of Morris Fuller Benton. Walter Tracy sums up my hostility to the deplorable Cheltenham in his book *The Typographic Scene*, 'Its lack of character and elegance ought to have repelled more people than it did'. One hopes that Bertram Goodhue, an architect, had a more felicitous touch with the design of buildings.

LAWRENCE WALLIS

abcdefghijklmnopqrstuvwxyz
ABCDEFGHIJKLMNOPQRSTUVWXYZ
1234567890 .,:;''«»ß&!?

abcdefghijklmnopqrstuvwxyz
ABCDEFGHIJKLMNOPQRSTUVWXYZ
1234567890 .,:;''«»ß&!?

Lawrence Wallis has an insatiable appetite for new Technological complexities which beset the printing and typesetting industries. He has worked with the Monotype Corporation and with Addressograph Multigraph, but his major contribution to them and to us must have been in the trade press in which he describes, explains and forecasts whatever he considers to be significant. He has also compiled reference books on terms and facts (glossaries & chronologies.) He has recently completed a study of the vain and now rather over-looked printer George W Jones. Lawrence on the other hand is modest but immensely energetic and well-informed, and surprisingly upbeat.
J D

DEA

Once upon a time, in the course of one of these international corporate takeovers that everybody hears about but that nobody understands, a huge German mining company called RWE acquired a slightly smaller German oil company going by the name of DEA from yet another huge international oil company named Texaco. To make the most of this new investment, a very well known advertising agency from New York was given the task of developing a progressive new corporate identity for the retail side of DEA's nationwide operations.

With a mere 6,500 typeface designs to choose from, it was perhaps inevitable that somebody would come up with the idea of using Helvetica as DEA's corporate typeface. However, once this momentous design solution had been decided upon, the designer showed himself also capable of a whole different mode of decision-making by deciding to choose the digital data needed for the font from URW's massive Digital Type Library.

Refusing to be tempted by any other of the 3000 or other designs we happen to have on offer, he picked out a weight of Berthold's Headline Helvetica and had it electronically slanted by 30 degrees, probably working to the theory of 'the larger the company, the greater the oblique angle'.

It is unfortunate for the German population of around 80 million people that DEA has some 1700 or more petrol filling stations dotted about the landscape of Germany, making this horrendous typographical monstrosity virtually unavoidable.

It is also unfortunate that good designers are more or less forced to accept low-cost jobs to make a living that, if they could afford the luxury, would never be taken on.

It is also unfortunate that a company is prepared to pay a lot of money for a lot of junk.

As for the DEA typeface design, you can really forget it!

PETER ROSENFELD

abcdefghijklmnopqrstuvwxyz

ABCDEFGHIJKLMNOPQRSTUVWXYZ

1234567890 .,:;'‘«»ß&!?

Just as Don Hase spent nearly all his working life with Alphatype, so do our first memories of Peter Rosenfeld bring us back to the days when, with Veronika Elsner, he was bringing the good news about a German product, Ikarus, to a country which tends to think that all development in an Easterly direction stops on Route 128, well short, even, of the Ambrose light. Even such development strongholds as Stanford, in the days when Don Knuth was showing us all TeX, acknowledged their achievements.

Peter's trouble was that he wasn't as nice to look at as Veronika. But few of us are.

Endeavour (Ashbee)

A type that is vapid and vile
Must be lacking in grace, wit and style:
If it fails in all three
Then it's obvious to me
That Endeavour's a miss by a mile.

JOHN DREYFUS

And his mother said unto him, Upon 13
me be thy curse, my son: only obey my
voice, and go fetch me them. And he 14

There is little in the world of printing and typesetting, in the whole business of graphic arts in the last fifty years or more that has not been touched by the influence of John Dreyfus. A founder member of ATypI and its second President, his work as the typographic adviser to Monotype, his long standing relationship with the Pierpont Morgan library and many other American institutions, his numerous books, his willingness and ability to correct all our prose, each of these occupations is almost a career in itself, and many of them have been recognised as such. At one time or another he has received nearly every award in the business. But here for the first time you learn that he was the model for Dorian Gray, and his ageless appearance is matched by a portrait in his flat of such unbelievable antiquity that even Methuselah is said to be put out by its existence.

Epic Bold Looking ..

Drop Shadow Outline
It has long been fashionable to regale apprentices and those new to the craft
of typography with tales of how it was in the days of hot metal! It must be
high time now that that particular ghost be laid to rest and replaced by the
days of Filmotype, Typositor and the scalpel. How was it you ask? Well, it
was hell. Not a normal hell but a particular and peculiar kind. Let me paint a
picture for you:
The next job in the rack has been there for some time, everyone has
seemingly been avoiding it. It's now turned into a panic and the overseer has
snarled that you immediately pick it up and get your finger out. This is not
conducive to the creative process, but these are the guys who pay the wages
so you gingerly pick it up.
You immediately realise why it's been lying there all afternoon – it's a locking
drop shadow headline job. Now, you're in a darkroom with eight other guys,
chemicals are everywhere, including on the floor, and the whole area is
bathed in a dim red light. Oh, and it's hot, as air conditioning has not reached
the slave level class yet.
The setting of a locking drop shadow on the Typositor requires manual
dexterity, a fit and supple body and the reactions of a ferret after a rabbit.
You sit there braced – the main film reel is threaded through the lens
assembly and an eery image of the first character is projected through a
plastic block onto liquids coating the photographic paper. Over your left
shoulder snakes the mask reel that allows you to offset those parts of the
main image that require the subsequent exposure from the film reel that lies
over your right shoulder that create the shadow effect, locking of course – are
you with me still? The delicate positioning of the initial character is
confirmed and the exposure is made, a shaft of light beams through the
sandwich of films held tightly in register by your left hand, the image quickly
appears under the plastic block and is made positive. The right hand
feverishly brings the shadow film reel into position and having found a clear
aperture on the main film reel positions the shadow with the aid of any offset
from the left hand reel only to find that both hands are in use and the
exposure must be made very soon. At this point the stress is beginning to tell
and the sweat is pouring off. The overseer pops in and asks for progress on
the job, you engage his help in pressing the exposure button only for him to
ask 'Why?'.
This is the first letter, there are twenty seven more and some fool now asks if

the client shouldn't have asked for it separated and on film. In the meantime more liquids are swirling on the floor and you feel something osmotically creeping into your sneakers through the hole in the left toe, you dare not move in case something in the delicate position of things moves.

You know that this is something you can look back on as part of a typographic learning experience but there again, is it not something best forgotten ...

DES EDMONDS

Des Edmonds must have been drinking from the same cup as John Dreyfus. It was in 1963 that the design group for which he was working first turned to Photocomposition as a business on the side, a suitable tail for a healthy dog. Within a short time, if the tail began to wag the dog, it was largely due to the knowledge and skill that Des brought to the company. Part of his success was that he was omniverous when it came to knowledge, and part of the success of those of us who were his competitors was because he would share this knowledge.

What makes him so supremely unpopular now is that while the rest of his contemporaries set about life as befits people of our great age and appearance, Des looks and acts as young as he ever did. But we continue to hope that he will one day break a limb ski-ing and be obliged to learn about a different pace, and sedentary pursuits, for at least a short while.

Folio

One of the Grotesk typefaces I'd like to see on the Graveyard of Type is Folio. The first weights of Folio were done in the same years as those of Helvetica. According to the famous Berthold E2 catalogue, Folio Light and Medium were released in 1957, whereas Helvetica Medium was released in 1958. Comparing the release dates of the condensed versions, it's the other way round: Folio Bold Condensed was first issued in 1956, but Helvetica Medium Condensed (by that time known as Haas Grotesk) was released in 1940. We therefore cannot say that the one is a copy from the other, but we can clearly see that hard competition was going on between the foundries to get the best sans serif on the market. Berthold expanded the range of its Akzidenz Grotesk (first weights released in 1896 and 1898) in 1053 and 1058 with two more weights of condensed as well as an expanded version in 1957. But this is not the point. What I like about Akzidenz Grotesk is that the design is not too 'smooth'. One can imagine that in the fifties somebody dug out the drawings (that were more truly revived as Akzidenz Old Face) and polished them up a bit for phototypesetting, but tried to preserve the flavour of the original. On the other hand Günter Gerhard Lange worked over the complete family into Akzidenz Grotesk Buch between 1969 and 1973 in order to have a Berthold face that could keep up with Helvetica and Univers. Helvetica was liked by (almost) everybody in the 60s and 70s, as a sort of 'typeface for the common man'. It seemed to breathe an atmosphere of new revolutionary simplicity. Univers (Haas 1957) was something for the distinguished typographer. It was superb, clean, complete (and had the best sans serif ampersand one had ever seen). Nobody ever did better than this (in fact: him: Adrian Frutiger). I still feel the pain when I found out that some engineers (may they go namelessly forever) had chopped up the 65 and 66 to make them match to the widths of the 55 and 56 for the linecaster and other inferior (opto-mechanical) devices based on the same ignorant technique that only allowed one width-table per four fonts. Yes! The ingenious numbering system! No more confusion about the 'medium' weight, was it 'halbfett' or 'normal'.

So many interesting things to tell about these typefaces, so what about Folio? Maybe you should ask yourselves: 'What can I say about it? Do I like it? Am I using it? Do I know somebody who is using it?' I bet that most people reading this will answer these questions with 'no'. Maybe you remember vaguely that this must have been the typeface with the a of which the upper half of the loop was far too thin in all weights, you tried to retouch it in the camera-ready paste ups in headline that contemporarily ran over two pages (just like the picture). Maybe you even have some left-over dry transfer sheets in your drawer with Folio Medium Numerals in sixty-six point (remember that there was no sheet with the other characters in the same size?) I guess that this is what it's all about.

ALBERT JAN POOL

abcdefghijklmnopqrstuvwxyz
ABCDEFGHIJKLMNOPQRSTUVWXYZ
1234567890 .,:;''«»ß&!?

abcdefghijklmnopqrstuvwxyz
ABCDEFGHIJKLMNOPQRSTUVWXY
1234567890 .,:;''«»ß&!?

Albert Jan, like Petr van Blokland and Peter Matthias Noordzij, was, and is, a key member of what we like to think of as the Dutch mafia, the unmistakably bright alumni of Gerrit's classes in Holland. For the past few years he has been digging himself in at Peter Karow's URW in Hamburg, where most of the pioneering work on outline technology was started in response to the needs of the late Walter Brendel.

Helvetica

Helvetica was the typeface of the Swiss movement begun at the Basel
Kunstgewerbeschule in the fifties. Slowly it seeped out through multinational
corporate identity (Knoll comes to mind) to become the face of bland
corporate stolidity (Bank of America). With the advent of the personal
computer, instead of being gracefully retired, Helvetica spread further like
Velveeta cheese, and its fifties look became ubiquitous in the sixties, seventies
and eighties. When the US government enacted legislation to create generic
packaging of essential items, the labelling face was also generic: Helvetica.
Based on nineteenth century grotesques, the main problem with Helvetica is
the fact that discrete shapes of the individual letters obstruct legibility. The
letters are square and squat, and don't communicate with their neighbours.
There is no airflow in words, and no cohesion of ideational units. As it is
generally set, there is more internal space in the counters than around the
words, creating ugly and standoffish silhouettes.
Velveetica is difficult to distinguish from many other types, such as Univers.
(Though people say, 'Of course they're different. Just look at the figure 2!' or
some such.) Adrian Frutiger, creator of Univers, revisited the sans serif for his
signage for Orly airport in Paris. The new improved Frutiger sans is not a
grot but a humanist-derived version, more like Gill Sans or Syntax, eminently
more readable because of the variety in letter-shapes, the openness of the
characters, the improved letterfit and, hence, the better aerodynamic shape of
the words. Velveetica wasn't a good type to begin with. There are many worse
text types, but Helvetica's very pervasiveness is a big stroke against it. It's
not invisible, just boring.

ALASTAIR JOHNSTON

abcdefghijklmnopqrstuvwxyz
ABCDEFGHIJKLMNOPQRSTUVWXYZ
1234567890 .,:;''«»ß&!?

abcdefghijklmnopqrstuvwxyz
ABCDEFGHIJKLMNOPQRSTUVWXYZ
1234567890 .,:;''«»ß&!?

*Presenting a little book that he and Frances Butler had made at the Poltroon
Press in San Francisco, Alastair Johnston once addressed a dinner at Queens
College Cambridge. In his talk we learned, via Mark Twain, that in Mark
Twain's early life in a newspaper office a man who could set 700 ems an hour
could put on any airs he wanted to. But he also told us that some New York
compositors, on a wager, had set 2000 ems an hour of minion for four hours at a
stretch. Minion, as you all know, was just a little over 7pt, and these men were
therefore picking up around four thousand very small pieces of type in an hour
and arranging them in a stick. That is more than one a second, and they had to
be selected in order!*

*It seems to me that there are more Scots out of Scotland than there are Scots in
Scotland. But it also seems to me that they are more erudite than the rest of us.
'Ideational' you will have to look up for yourselves.*

Helvetica

Of all the typefaces I've been connected with, one stands out through its omnipresence, in bad versions and good, used well, used poorly, but used, used, used until abused. A year or so after its US introduction, my heart rose as I realized how quickly it showed signs of becoming a true standard. Riding in a Manhattan elevator, I glanced at the inspection certificate; badly printed, smudged, grimy, there it was, even on this card.

In the early sixties the Linotypes we still built at Mergenthaler set perhaps sixty percent of the world's alphabetic type, largely with the matrices we made. Cutting a new design was a hugely expensive and time consuming process. A dimensioned engineering drawing was required for each character at each size or group of sizes. It controlled the cutting of pattern and punch, striking of the punch into brass matrices, and over forty steps of their machining. A Linotype font of one point size was made up of ninety different characters in two duplexed weights, typically fifteen hundred matrices to provide enough of each to compose two or three lines. Loading such a magazine onto the machine was no job for the weak. Price was roughly five hundred dollars a size, up to ten thousand dollars for a complete series to equip a single machine.

Six to fourteen point with Italic and with Bold took over two years to prepare, and cost millions in today's dollars. We worked on an architectural scale. Those of us who made the decisions tended to think of ourselves as great architects. That such heroic decisions were dictated by the slowness and expense of our cumbersome technology didn't strike us. Guardians of public taste, we decided what few faces were truly suitable for heavy public use, and cut only typefaces we judged attractive to major portions of the industry two years hence and for some years thereafter. We damned as a 'fad' any typeface of less than massive appeal. We serviced the market with as few major series of broad appeal as possible. Special linecaster faces for individual customers were rare. The proprietors of General Motors Gothic enquired about the cost of putting it onto the machine, but never replied to my estimate.

The system inevitably created a few popular standards. 'Can we get it on the machine?' was the question asked at any serious choice of typeface. In the sixties, by cutting it for the Linotype, we made Helvetica the Swiss sans serif of choice across most of the world. Omnipresence of the design began to bore. We passed through a stage where every new photographic typesetter operated on its own unique principles. To compete, each of the many photographic contenders had to prepare in its own peculiar font format a growing group of

A little later Lludd had the length and breadth of the island measured and found its centre to be in Oxford. There he had a pit dug, and in the pit he set a vat of the *best mead that could be made, with a silk sheet over the vat, and he himself watched that night and saw the dragons fighting.* When they were tired and worn out they sank onto the sheet and dragged it down to the bottom of the vat, where they drank up the mead and fell asleep. Lludd wrapped the sheet round them and locked them in a stone chest in the most secure place he could find.

standard designs to form the heart of another all-but-identical library, starting with Helvetica and Times.

Linotype refused to license Helvetica to Berthold for text machines. Hoffmann had written that he had improved Berthold's Akzidenz to arrive at Helvetica; Berthold improved Akzidenz too, and released Akzidenz Book, a real refinement of Helvetica. Linotype prepared 'Linotype New Helvetica' in reply. As tired of the face as a designer might be, these improvements brought a smile.

Compugraphic cut Helios time and again, finally producing an acceptable cut in CG Triumvirate. Adobe cut its typographic teeth on an awkward version licensed by Linotype in spite of all-too-visible potatoes lurking inside the sack-like shapes of the Bold. These, and others like them, hit new records for volume. One grew truly sick of the repetition.

We have progressed to a digital plateau where a single imagesetting technology, shared in common, is replacing the variety of competing typesetting methods. Character outlines defined in mathematical splines produce the dot patterns required for each size on all digital devices. The baker's dozen of look-alike libraries are being rushed into the two great public formats that now service all major platforms interchangeably: Type One and TrueType. Standard designs are offered ever more cheaply in an unprecedented price war.

Cost of producing a new typeface has dropped nearly a thousandfold from hot metal days; what we measured in millions is now measured in thousands. Time to do it has dropped nearly a hundredfold; what we did in years is now finished in weeks. Specials for publications and companies proliferate. A playful, witty design is no longer a 'fad', but can be next month's topical hit, turning an immediate profit. Heavy industry becomes a fashion playground. Insistence on standard designs lightens. Variation is easily created and lightly documented.

To the weary designer, Helvetica seems best forgotten, although some distant morning it may surprise and refresh us by offering relief from the insistence of new favorites. Never again should we have to endure quite such dulling repetition of any single design.

MIKE PARKER

abcdefghijklmnopqrstuvwxyz
ABCDEFGHIJKLMNOPQRSTUVWXYZ
1234567890 .,:;"'«»ß&!?

There are probably some people who remember Mike Parker from before he went to Linotype. To the rest of us he was Linotype and Bitstream, and very visible. He has now gravitated to the ideal climate of San Diego and acquired a better half as far diagonally from him as you can get in the United States, tucked away in the northern reaches of New England.

It is pleasant to be reminded that Mike was a scholar before he was a type founder, and it is also pleasant to be reminded that Edouard Hoffmann is as worthy to be credited with Helvetica (and Haas Clarendon and Anzeigen Grotesk) as Stanley Morison is to be with Times New Roman. In fact, if we look at the evidence now coming out of Lanston Monotype archives, perhaps he deserves it rather more.

But then he must also share the blame.

(ITC) Lubalin Graph

The idea of sticking slabs onto a sans serif typeface at all seems silly, even contrived— as if a serif is an accessory for type to wear or not, depending upon the whim of a designer. (ITC) Lubalin Graph is a particularly irksome case in point. (ITC) Avant Garde Gothic, whose value (or lack of) to the typographic lexicon can be debated on its own, does not, to my mind, offer an appropriate host on which to graft club feet. This is essentially what Herb did to create his namesake design. ('Lubalin's Graft' would have been more apropos.) Unfortunately, this is the only design which many type faddists will attribute to Mr Lubalin, which is a pity given his masterful handling (nay, invention) of the American advertising type aesthetic of the 1970s. Technically, the problems arise from a lack of sympathy between character shapes, slabs, and attendant counters, crotches and fillets. Aesthetically, the issue is whether a graphic effect is worth making a whole typeface statement over. And for those who dismiss Avant Garde Gothic as an overly contrived, geometric design to begin with, these two wrongs certainly don't make a right. I must also confess to a personal reason for my vendetta against this face – I employed it shamelessly in one of my early graphic design projects that went horribly awry. I thought it would be neat to set a brochure's text copy in Lubalin Graph, surprinted along with illustrations over real technical graph paper. I'm certain that no one but me was interested in the pun, and the effect was marginally readable and overdone. Even if it is true that 'there is no such thing as a bad typeface, only a bad use of it,' I would feel safer about other designers not being challenged with Lubalin Graph's appropriate use.

GARRETT BOGE

abcdefghijklmnopqrstuvwxyz
ABCDEFGHIJKLMNOPQRSTUVWXYZ
1234567890 .,:;'«»ß&!?

abcdefghijklmnopqrstuvwxyz
ABCDEFGHIJKLMNOPQRSTUVWXYZ
1234567890 .,:;'«»ß&!?

People march to different drums. Few had the good fortune to find a drum that
brought them a small design studio in Gig Harbor in the State of Washington,
where they could be paid both to design graphics and make fonts.
It must have taken some heavy bribery to get him to leave, even to an office so
well placed overlooking Puget Sound as that of Elseware. Here he now helps them
with their elastic fonts, that newest and perhaps most frightening of the options
that the computer has brought to type manufacture.

Lydian

Ugh! Fingernails scraping on a chalk board, visual inanity, ugliness given credibility by age alone. There's no excuse for such a meaningless design, and all the more astounding that a foundry took the time to cut it in metal. It is neither fish nor fowl, not a script, not a Roman, not a text, not a display. Its dithering leaves it strident on a page, at odds with every other design, incapable of smooth companionship with other typefaces.

Is it a calligraphic? Only in the bad dreams of Arrighi. It is featureless, emotionless, foolish in its simplistic shape. It means nothing, intuits nothing, lies there a dead thing, making everything around it dead too.

Legende is real, and Optima is real. Give me Delphian or give me death! But please, oh please, don't set it in Lydian! Hammer Uncial and Solemnis at least have a design, while Lydian is worse than the most basic schoolchild's primer. Boring, obsequious Lydian!

Horrors, it makes a chill on my spine. Because you are neither hot nor cold, humanistic or machine, because your form defies any known organic or inorganic design, I spew you out of my mouth, and condemn you to eternity in the outer darkness of forgotten typefaces. Good riddance!

CYNTHIA HOLLANDSWORTH

abcdefghijklmnopqrstuvwxyz
ABCDEFGHIJKLMNOPQRSTUVWXYZ
1234567890 .,:;''«»ß&!?

abcdefghijklmnopqrstuvwxyz
ABCDEFGHIJKLMNOPQRSTUVWXYZ
1234567890 .,:;''«»ß&!?

There are few people more visible, in every sense of the word, than Cynthia. She has been a moving spirit in what may be the fruitless quest for legislation that could protect typeface design in a commercial world, because this is where expediency appears to carry more weight that morality.
She also appears to have been landed with the permanent job of chairing the PostScript users group bi-annual meeting which is known as the Font Free for all. She is a striking woman who can easily be distinguished at as much as 400 paces by even the myopic. But she has at least one fault. Nobody should be allowed to construct a piece of prose that includes a verb like intuit.

One Up, One Up Outline

Way back in the swinging sixties, when my youthful soul was consumed by enthusiasm, if not naked ambition, I was surprised and delighted to have my first typeface design Westminster accepted by Robert Norton of Photoscript Limited, for publication in his photo-typesetting catalogue. Spurred on by the regular appearance of royalty payments, I produced several further typeface designs. Most of these ideas were properly strangled at birth. One Up unfortunately survived to become a complete font. Looking at it now, I feel much as I imagine a mature filmstar must feel when, 30-odd years after the event, she comes across photographs of herself as a struggling starlet, revealing all for the readers of some popular girlie magazine.
I wish I hadn't done it.

LEO MAGGS

ABCDEFGHIJK
LMNOPQRSTU
abcdefghijklmn
rstuvwxyz-%!?

Some designers seem to successfully hoe their row attended by the same loyal clients as one decade follows another, impervious to the fluctuations of the economy and the various fiscal disasters brought upon us by ambitious politicians. Their knowledge is considerable and many of them therefore teach on a part time basis and bring to their students a strong sense of quality, and the consequent ability to distinguish between what is ephemeral and what must endure. Leo Maggs is such a one.

Palatino

Palatino, that elegant text face, deserves a holiday. We're forgetting how it ought to look. We see the characters everywhere, output coarsely from the ubiquitous laser printer. Unfortunately, these letters are stubby hints of the real thing.

Thus over (and badly) used, the face has lost its luster, which is too bad. Palatino repays the small effort needed to set it effectively – some leading, a generous proportion of line measure to type size – but designers seem to be avoiding it for serious work.

Any typeface can fall out of synch with the taste of the times, but Palatino hasn't suffered that more or less natural fate – it has been debased, almost accidentally, by the technology. Perhaps a holiday will revive it.

KATHLEEN TINKEL

abcdefghijklmnopqrstuvwxyz
ABCDEFGHIJKLMNOPQRSTUVWXYZ
1234567890 .,:;'"«»ß&!?

abcdefghijklmnopqrstuvwxyz
ABCDEFGHIJKLMNOPQRSTUVWXYZ
1234567890 .,:;'"«»ß&!?

Don't try to impress Kathleen with a bad typeface. A mediocre typeface might be forgiven if it were wrapped around the label of a particularly good bottle of wine. Actually, it's difficult to begin a description of Kathleen without resorting immediately to 'typefaces and wine'. After all, where is she usually found? We all meet at odd points on the globe for tradeshows, conferences, and such – but really, mostly for dinner. In real life, she is a prolific author, reporting on and grumbling about electronic typography, publishing, and prepress. One can only assume she does so because the field of reporting on fine cuisine is so crowded. Kathleen once explained to me why she spends so much time with fonts – she said something along the lines of 'I write about prepress issues because it's my livelihood; I hang around this other crowd simply because I so love the type'.

Park Avenue

I'd love to say I detest Park Avenue, but I don't want my name associated with it.

abcdefghijklmnopqrstuvwxyz

ABCDEFGHIJKLMNOPQRST

UVWXYZ 1234567890 .,:;" «»ß&!?

If there is a more prolific writer on desk-top publishing in the United States than Daniel Will-Harris, it could only be because somebody else is writing under two different names. Not only will you find many of his books in every bookshop, but there will also be few weeks where you won't also find an article of his in one of the many journals which cater to the need we all have of wanting to find out how to use more of the tools that we buy.

Rockwell

When I started work, in the spring of 1949, at Methuen, I had the responsibility for all the jackets turned out by the firm – several hundred new books and even more reprints and new editions.

All the jackets were printed letterpress. Fiction usually had four-colour halftone blocks. Everything else was printed from type, often in a single colour. I designed them all. I had no qualifications whatsoever; my only relevant experience, by no means to be sneezed at, was a couple of weeks in the Aylesbury Composing Room, hand-setting ads for magazines.

I got hold of type-specimen books from all and sundry, and was soon experimenting like crazy; Chisel was the modish display face that year, I recall. I learned my way around by studying the form in Denny's bookshop in the Strand, and from people like Lynton Lamb, from whom I picked up the sterling virtues of Cloister Black. But masses of printer-binders were restricted to Monotype faces, so I used Perpetua and Times Roman lavishly, often including many rules and borders.

One thing puzzled me greatly. Every Monotype house had in their type-book Rockwell in many sizes. Whoever had been in charge of Monotype sales when Rockwell had been introduced had done a fantastic job. Everybody had it. In those days, I could identify almost any display face at once. But I never saw Rockwell used by anybody. I felt sorry for it, and tried to find a good excuse for using it, and got to the proof stage once or twice. But I never managed to use Rockwell, any more than anybody else. It was too awful.

NIGEL VINEY

abcdefghijklmnopqrstuvwxyz
ABCDEFGHIJKLMNOPQRSTUVW
XYZ 1234567890 .,:;''«»ß&!?

abcdefghijklmnopqrstuvwxyz
ABCDEFGHIJKLMNOPQRSTUVWXYZ
1234567890 .,:;''«»ß&!?

*The publishing and printing industry in Britain seems to have been overrun by
Vineys, a collection of intellectual eminences grises controlling matters discreetly
from the Chiltern Hills. Younger sons, I suspect, instead of being sent to the army
or the Church, were sternly dispatched to London by their mothers to add tone to
what might otherwise be a fairly scruffy publishing industry. Presumably, as the
Vineys have always married wisely – and Nigel is certainly no exception – the
mothers were also instructing the publishing sons to keep orders coming to the
printing sons.*
*We are all a bit jealous that at this stage of his working life Nigel, having
returned to Buckinghamshire from the publishing industry in London, seems to
have found angels who are now continually shovelling money at him to make
books that most of us would happily have made for love.*

Romulus Sloping Roman

T · & · S · HARTZ

26
6

Dear Robert,
A difficult question.
I thought about it for a
long time. After all, I think
that the sloping roman of
Van Krimpen would do.
It was made on the instigation
of Morison. It was the
only variation they could
think of, and a sad
mistake. Especially I think
because VK was, in a way,
a very rigid sort of man
& he had no example to
fight shy of. How is Gail
& her beautifull daughter,
what luck they are not like
you. Love Sem.

SEM HARTZ

ABCDEFGHIJKLMNOPQRSTU
abcdefghijklmnopqrstuvwxyz
1234567890

Sem Hartz has the coordination of hand and mind which has made him a first-class shot, a brilliant engraver of banknotes and postage stamps, a bold sailor and confident designer of stamps. He developed a peculiarly English sense of humour while in hiding while his country was occupied by the German Army in World War II. Confined between the floorboards of the house where he hid, he listened avidly to the BBC, especially to the comedian Tommy Handley. Life at Enschedé en Zonen was less comic, but Sem lightened the mood. He complained that the Pope stole his best joke. When asked how many people worked at Enschedé, Sem replied 'About half of them.'
J D

Romulus Sloping Roman

In an article entitled 'Towards an Ideal Italic' which appeared in *The Fleuron* (Volume V., 1926) Stanley Morison surmised, after much prefatory supposition that 'The perfect italic is ... a slanted roman.' Morison came to this rather remarkable and arguable conclusion after stating as fact (and, in italics) that '... the essential quality of "italic" ... is a certain informality' and that '... the quality of slope is no true test of an "italic".' He then proceeded to turn these statements on their heads in order to prove (and I must paraphrase his rather lengthy arguments) that, since the only function of italic type was to support the roman and that italic could only do this if it had 'sufficient differential indications' which 'must be kept to the minimum, ... we require an upright roman for our text and a slanted roman as a secondary type.' Walter Tracy, commenting on this idea many years later said (with tongue firmly in cheek, I think) 'it seemed at the time a revelation of truth and was taken seriously.'

The first example of Morison's theory being put into practice (partially, at least) can be seen in the italic of Eric Gill's Perpetua type. The most extreme application can be seen here in Jan Van Krimpen's design of Romulus Sloped Roman. In later years, the theoretician and the designer both had regrets: 'the argument in favour of a sloped roman was perhaps carried too far' and ' ... we both found that we had been mistaken.'

Interestingly, the sloped-roman italic of Romulus appeared at almost the same time as the one designed by W A Dwiggins for his Electra typeface. Soon afterwards (due, I am certain, to negative reaction) Electra 'Italic' was supplemented by a 'true italic' design called Cursive (which is quite good). No such remedy was ever offered for the 'mistake' of Romulus Sloped Roman.

So forget sloped roman. I find it most intriguing that Morison was so hell-bent on proving himself, his theory, or both, that he dismissed the idea of an italic type which preserved the informality of the cursive hand but had little, if any, slope (ie. an 'Upright Italic') – even though he illustrates his article with several examples of such hands and comments on their 'elegance and freedom'.

JEFF LEVEL

ABCDEFGHIJKLMNOPQRSTU
abcdefghijklmnopqrstuvwxyz
1234567890

Jeff Level sees himself as a schizophrenic. Half his life has been pulled towards type. Half his mind is still being pulled towards wine. His knowledge on both subjects is immense. But what he probably won't acknowledge is the fact that his eye may be better than that of anybody contributing to this book. It takes a special skill to know within thousandths of an inch on a drawing three or four inches high that there is a mistake in the drawing that must be corrected if that letter is to be part of an alphabet whose other drawings are on separate pieces of paper. Now that so many typefaces are made on the resolution of a television screen this may be a skill that will disappear.

Satanick

My recollection of a type I'd consider best forgotten goes back over a half century when I was still an undergraduate in college in the 1920s. At that time I had no inkling I'd choose to become a printer. I was interested in books as literature rather than as works of art. I then came under the persuasive guidance of Alice Millard. Her late husband, George Madison Millard, had presided for several decades over the rare book *Saints and Sinners Corner* of the McClurg's Book Store in Chicago. It was the favorite haunt of writers and book collectors of that area during the years of the turn of the century. In his yearly forays to England in search of rare and precious books Millard had become acquainted with William Morris who was just beginning to create his Kelmscott Press books. Millard was mightily impressed with them and was probably the first dealer to introduce these books to American collectors. After his retirement from McClurg's, he and his young bride moved to California where the two of them continued selling rare books, especially Kelmscott Press books, to discriminating local collectors. As a result there are more Kelmscott books in collections and libraries in California than any place with the exception of England. Alice Millard introduced me to these books along with T J Cobden-Sanderson's Doves Press books which influenced me into choosing to become a printer. In time I came to recognize the shortcomings of Morris' types while approving of their use in his robust books. The clone which the American Typefounders cast with the name Satanick I felt was an effrontery to Morris, especially as they applied to copyright it. So this is the type I have selected to be forgotten. But I am undoubtedly too late. It has already been.

WARD RITCHIE

Persons with bright thoughts and aspiring minds seem from the very earliest part of the 16th Century to have been dissatisfied 🦎 🦎 🦎 🦎 🦎

Though Ward Ritchie hailed from the typographically fertile state of California, he turned up in Paris in his late twenties on the door step of the great artist-printer Schmied, who took Ward under his wing. The consequences of that friendly act are still discernible in Ward's typographic and gastronomic taste: both are robust and ever open to new experiments. After a successful career with his own commercial printing shop and his own publishing ventures with cookery books, as well as a great deal of freelance book design for California University Press, he retired to start his own private press on the Pacific coast at Laguna Bay, operating an Albion hand press under the imprint of Imprenta Verde. He remains as inventive as he was in the twenties, and still writes up his journal in which he has recorded more typographical experiences than most of his contemporaries. There is nowhere to be found a more genial and generous figure than Ward, and few have such a wide range of talents.
JD

Schelter-Antiqua

If I genuinely don't like a face, I usually prefer to say nothing at all about it. Here, I will discuss a face for which I have a sneaking admiration, even though I feel duty bound to dislike it because it runs contrary to all the rules of good design that I was taught as a student of calligraphy and typography. This is Schelter-Antiqua and its companion Schelter-Kursiv, cut at the J G Schelter and Giesecke foundry in Leipzig. I don't know their exact date of release, but it had to be prior to 1914, because, as G. Willem Ovink pointed out, these faces were clearly the starting point for Morris Fuller Benton's design of Souvenir, released by ATF in 1914. But Benton did not make an exact copy. Schelter-Antiqua is a peculiar hybrid of art-nouveau with gothic (in the sense of 'broken-script', not sans-serif). The capitals have soft, sinuous Jugendstil forms, but while the lower-case sometimes has similarly supple features, it often paradoxically shows abrupt, textura-like breaks in the x-line terminals and arches. In Schelter-Kursiv, the lower-case is somewhat softer. The Antiqua and Kursiv were not the only members of the family. The Antiqua appeared in several variations and, in addition, Schelter & Giesecke showed several closely related designs, (Leipziger Lateinschrift for example) although these are so close to the Schelter-Antiqua and Kursiv styles that today we might consider them only minor variations on the theme, not separate typefaces.

In *Asymmetric Typography* (the 1967 English translation of his *Typographische Gestaltung* of 1935), Jan Tschichold shows an advertising page from the German printing magazine, Deutsche Buch und Steindrucker, in which much of the text is composed in Schelter-Antiqua, Kursiv, and other members of their family. Tschichold's caption states, 'Example of German typography (1922) before the advent of Jan Tschichold's New Typography. Disgust with such degenerate type faces and arrangements led the author to attempt to eradicate them entirely.' But he was not entirely successful.

From the Schelter-Antiqua and Kursiv designs Benton extracted the art nouveau forms but discarded the gothic. His Souvenir is more of a single coherent concept, without the peculiar dissonance of the disparate elements of the Schelter cuttings. I recall Mike Parker once proclaiming that Benton's Souvenir is a good example of one of the few typeface plagiarisms in which the design was actually improved in the process. Although Souvenir languished in the ATF catalog for half a century, Ed Benguiat's refinement of the face for ITC and photocomposition brought the design into the mainstream of American culture in the 1970's. To Benton's design, shown in a single light weight of roman in the ATF 1923 specimen book, Benguiat added an italic based on the roman of Souvenir, not on the Schelter-Kursiv, and several bolder weights, while retaining the basic letter shapes. For a decade or more, Souvenir seemed to be used almost everywhere across the country, and perhaps nowhere was it more popular than in the menus of the vast lower stratum of restaurants, where its 'dipped-in-chocolate' pretzel look seemed to promise Americans meals without risk, none of the dangerously spiky serifs of Times Roman, nor the rock-hard, jaw-breaking geometry of Helvetica. Souvenir was really something you could sink your teeth into.

CHUCK BIGELOW

Moderne Gedichte
Sonnenbäder
HEINES WERKE

It is difficult to know what we should think of Chuck Bigelow. There are those who think of him as a teacher. Certainly the West Coast of the United States is thickly inlaid with many of his ex-students busily shaping the way that California is going to influence type and graphic design. He is a born teacher, with an immense memory that makes it easy for him to draw on examples to illustrate his points. He may think of himself as a type designer. Certainly the Lucida family, which grows like Topsy, is very close to his heart.

I think of both him and Kris Holmes as prisoners in a rose nursery. Pots used to be as far as the eye could see, wherever there was a flat space in reach of the garden hose. Now, in their new house, the eye can see nearly as far as Japan, and the pots have reverted to scale.

Serifa/Glypha

Perhaps a typeface that should never have arrived was Serifa,
or was it Glypha?
And that's the point, I never can tell!
(Sorry Adrian, as I do love your typefaces –
and I am always using Frutiger).

ALAN SHELLEY

abcdefghijklmnopqrstuvwxyz
ABCDEFGHIJKLMNOPQRSTUVWXYZ
1234567890 .,:;''«»ß&!?

abcdefghijklmnopqrstuvwxyz
ABCDEFGHIJKLMNOPQRSTUVWXYZ
1234567890 .,:;''«»ß&!?

All sorts of people have come and gone from the Linotype subsidiary at Cheltenham. Cheltenham has had periods when they were pulling in money as though it was free, and there were also times when perhaps the company was suffering from having threatened the role of subsidiaries in other countries. Through all these years we have all sat, from time to time, near the slightly hunched figure of Alan Shelley, at one of those committee meetings that form so large a part of our working lives.
There are few of us on the circuit who do not hold fond memories of his thoughtful rustic voice, and wise words.

Souvenir

What I have said about Souvenir over the last 16 years goes beyond character assassination: Real men don't set Souvenir. Souvenir is a font fatale. 'Souvenir: The Movie' – An amorphous blob from another planet with puce antennae and green skin invades earth and infiltrates the advertising world. Within a few years it advances to creative director and blends right in. Congress has selected Souvenir as their official typeface. I only know what I read in the trade press, and it scares the Souvenir out of me. Souvenir Outline: a gutless typeface. We could send Souvenir to Mars but there are international treaties on pollution in outer space. We can only pollute the earth. So far our planet is the only toxic waste dump in the solar system. The United Nations has declared the earth a Souvenir free zone. Souvenir: punk type. There's nothing wrong with Souvenir that a complete re-design would not cure. The Ayatollah says that anyone who uses Souvenir is an insult and should be eliminated. Souvenir: Madonna's favorite typeface. It is now official: Souvenir will be cryogenically frozen and placed in a time capsule for a future when a cure may be found. Clinton is naming a Design Czar to cabinet rank, who will prepare a national strategy to combat bad design. A campaign is being developed with the theme 'Souvenir—Just say No!' Souvenir: Smurf typography. Archaeologists have discovered that Stonehenge is actually a prehistoric publishing system. When viewed from two miles above it resembles a Souvenir lowercase o. It is a dimension of serif and sans, of time and type between light and drop shadow. You are on a voyage into the graffiti of the human mind. You have entered the Souvenir Zone. Souvenir: stealth typography. It is now official: Adobe will introduce a PostScript RIP that is so fast, running at full speed would slow down the rotation of the earth, sending Souvenir back in time. A medieval printer would then look at the font and remark 'That is grotesque', and change typographic terminology forever. There should be at least a seven day waiting period before you use Souvenir. Remember: Friends don't let friends set Souvenir. Be a designated typographer. The bumper sticker of the week says: Souvenir happens.

FRANK ROMANO

abcdefghijklmnopqrstuvwxyz
ABCDEFGHIJKLMNOPQRSTUVW
XYZ 1234567890 .,:;''«»ß&!?

abcdefghijklmnopqrstuvwxyz
ABCDEFGHIJKLMNOPQRSTUVW
XYZ 1234567890 .,:;''«»ß&!?

There is a corner in the world of journalism that Frank Romano made all his own
when he began with Type World. When we agree with what he writes he is wise.
When we disagree he is, of course, thicker than two short planks. But we never
pass up the chance to see what he has to say, and it is for this reason that
advertisers still fight to place their ads near what he is writing.
Let us hope that his passage into Academia at the Rochester Institute of
Technology will in no way stem the flow from whatever PC he is using these days.

ITC Souvenir

A Terrible Typeface

What a bore. Not ITC Souvenir again. This typeface is nearly as boring as Helvetica or Times New Roman, so often do we see it in use.

For just about twenty years now, ITC Souvenir has been used in every conceivable application except when something really classical and elegant was called for. Even then some people have tried to use ITC Souvenir Light for this purpose.

Those that know about these things, and can spot the typeface and what it stands for have told me that it conjures up images best forgotten: The Disco typeface. A sort of 'Saturday Night Fever' typeface wearing tight white flared pants, mixed in with very definite and sugary overtones of 'The Sound of Music'.

Ladies and Gentlemen, I do believe that Elvis has left the building.

As we walk away quickly from these frankly upsetting images of almost now; walk away quickly along the empty concrete corridor, is it the Bee Gees I hear? No, no it's the thin echo of Andy William's crooning 'Moon River'. No it's not, its the Musak Version.

Still in the corridor, I round the corner and come out into the sunlight. A type expert is standing at a podium on a green lawn surrounded by bright and happy flowers. He is explaining that ITC Souvenir does not go well with some Old Style designs. Oh no, what a tragedy!

People are clustered on the path near the lawn looking confused. They have never noticed ITC Souvenir. It is everywhere but they cannot see it. It just makes them feel so good.

I wake with a start, I am at my desk: What a nightmare, a world just full of ITC Souvenir.

But you know, whatever anyone says, this makes ITC Souvenir one of a handful of the most notorious typefaces of all time.

MARK BATTY

abcdefghijklmnopqrstuvwxyz
ABCDEFGHIJKLMNOPQRSTUVW
XYZ 1234567890 .,:;''«»ß&!?

abcdefghijklmnopqrstuvwxyz
ABCDEFGHIJKLMNOPQRSTUVW
XYZ 1234567890 .,:;''«»ß&!?

abcdefghijklmnopqrstuvwxyz
ABCDEFGHIJKLMNOPQRSTUVW
XYZ 1234567890 .,:;''«»ß&!?

The task of coming to ITC after Aaron Burns is one that few would relish. ITC was always Aaron's company from the days when he first arrived in Bruges with Julius Bloom (was that really his name, or do I forget?) and Ed Gottschall. They came to make their presentations to the type founders gathered there. It cannot be easy to come to a company to replace somebody whom everybody loves.
One of the many reasons that his friends like Mark Batty is his courage and loyalty. But more than that is that he has absolutely no image of himself as an important person, a quality which those of us who find it sometimes difficult to be made fun of envy most dreadfully.

Souvenir

SOUVENIR! Souvenir of what I would like to know? A souvenir of every ghastly mistake ever made in type design gathered together – with a few never thought of before – into one execrable mish-mash. A more hideous rabble never straggled across a page. I went to the Monotype launch of this face (together with some others) in the mid 70s. Although I had consumed a fair quantity of their wine, I restrained the free flow of my feelings. I did, however, say to John Dreyfus that I was surprised that they had issued a type so far outside the fine tradition of the Monotype range. Even typography's ace diplomat paused for a moment before saying that it was a typeface that had its uses for certain sorts of advertising work. That was the best he could do. If this type had been cobbled together in a couple of hours under the influence of an emperor-sized hangover it would be bad enough. But this is a typeface saying 'everyone must recognise me instantly. The layman may not know boring old Times from boring old Centaur or boring old Ehrhardt from boring old Baskerville but I am so different that everyone will recognize me.' ANY author deserves better than Souvenir – even Barbara Cartland and I.

PETER GUY

A little later Lludd had the length and breadth of the island measured and found its centre to be in Oxford. There he had a pit dug, and in the pit he set a vat *of the best mead that could be made, with a silk sheet over the vat, and he himself watched that night and saw the dragons fighting.* When they were tired and worn out they sank onto the sheet and dragged it down to the bottom of the vat, where they drank up the mead and fell asleep. Lludd wrapped the sheet round them and locked them in a stone chest in the most secure place he could find.

Peter Guy has found time to practice as well as teach book design. He taught at Oxford, and designed some innovative books in London for the Folio Society. His panache is more noticeable in the size and style of his bow ties, but he invigorates the meetings of the several societies and clubs to which he belongs.
J D

Three Sans Italic ...

ITC Quay, Lucida Sans Italic and, heaven help me, Stone Sans Italic (just the lowercase b and p), could disappear and I, normally a lover of all things type, wouldn't mourn a bit. Why the hell is this mad man picking on some of his favorite type designers? Well, truth be known I have more than a little dislike, actually a large dislike for italic sans serif lowercases with tear-drop shaped counters in the a,b,d,p,q and sometimes g.

(I know where this dislike comes from but I didn't realize it until I blurted it out at an ITC type selection committee meeting. An alphabet was placed before me and I said 'I hate it, it's too much like Stone Sans.' There was a momentary hush over the group and then a loud and long 'Oooooh', the kind that follows some sort of sacrilege in a temple, from everyone at the table. I quickly shut up, went back to the studio and started pawing my way through specimens to see what it was that had caused this to occur.)

Well, truth be told, there is a masculine structure to sans serif a, b, d, p, q and g where the curve stem comes straight out of the straight stem and into the curve, like an arm coming out of a shoulder. This happens in faces like Franklin Gothic, Meta and many others. And there is the fully round, I think feminine, branching that occurs in Helvetica (except the Compressed), Futura and Antique Olive among others. Even in the Italics of these faces, these structures are of the feminine or masculine variety.

But the faces I mention as forgettable, are both. That is, they have feminine and masculine branching occurring in the same letters. So the a, b, d, p, q and sometimes g end up with these tear-dropped shaped contours that make me want to forget the whole damn font.

I still don't know why...

DAVID BERLOW

abcdefghijklmnopqrstuvwxyz
ABCDEFGHIJKLMNOPQRSTUVWXYZ
1234567890 .,:;"«»ß&!?

peter piper picked a peck of pickled peppers
bbbbob

We first learned to love Berlow when he was at Bitstream, when we could rely on him for ironic comments on whatever show or seminar we happened to be at. It became harder to love him as his career progressed and Font Bureau was started and shouldered its way into what is known as the 'leading edge' of font technology and it became clear that he was getting to know more than the rest of us. Perhaps the reason we are still delighted to eat with him is that he hasn't yet got round to rubbing our noses in it.

Univers

As every student of typography knows, the Roman alphabet, typified by the Trajan Column inscription in Rome (c. AD 114), is the foundation of all Western alphabets. When many nineteenth-century type founders eschewed classic Roman proportions in favour of alphabets whose capitals were of equal width, such as Thorowgood's sans serif designs of 1832, they rightly classified them 'Grotesques'.

Edward Johnston returned to the traditional Roman form when, in 1916, he produced his famous sans serif alphabet, which later became the exclusive lettering style of London Transport. Other sans faces, such as Koch's Cable and Renner's Futura, became available by the late nineteen-twenties; but it was Eric Gill who, in 1928, refined the sans serif into something near perfection, with Gill Sans.

Then along came the new technology of photo-typesetting. This gave us the capability to reproduce a full range of type sizes from a common original – often with disastrous results. Univers, designed by Frutiger in 1957 for the French type foundry Deberny & Peignot, boasted of being the first alphabet specifically designed as 'one image for all sizes'. For this alone, I grudgingly acknowledge its place in the history books. Univers reverts to the ugly uniformity of the Grotesques while Gill's Roman proportions are so much more elegant, and possessed of that essential quality Edward Johnston referred to as 'readableness'.

Block letters, lacking thick and thin strokes, really do need those variations of proportion which endow each letter with its recognizable form and character. Without them they become camouflaged by a word, and the words become camouflaged by the paragraph. Thus, not only is the elegance and beauty of the printed page dulled, but the whole process and pleasure of reading is impaired.

Down with Univers! Long live Gill Sans!

LEO MAGGS

abcdefghijklmnopqrstuvwxyz
ABCDEFGHIJKLMNOPQRSTUVWXYZ
1234567890 .,:;''«»ß&!?

abcdefghijklmnopqrstuvwxyz
ABCDEFGHIJKLMNOPQRSTUVWXYZ
1234567890 .,:;''«»ß&!?

Some designers seem to successfully hoe their row attended by the same loyal clients as one decade follows another, impervious to the fluctuations of the economy and the various fiscal disasters brought upon us by ambitious politicians. Their knowledge is considerable and many of them therefore teach on a part time basis and bring to their students a strong sense of quality, and the consequent ability to distinguish between what is ephemeral and what must endure. Leo Maggs is such a one.

Who Forgot

Who Remembered

abcdefghijklmnopqrstuvwxyz
ABCDEFGHIJKLMNOPQRSTUVWXYZ
1234567890 .,:;"«»ß&!?

abcdefghijklmnopqrstuvwxyz
ABCDEFGHIJKLMNOPQRSTUVWXYZ
1234567890 .,:;"«»ß&!?

abcdefghijklmnopqrstuvwxyz
ABCDEFGHIJKLMNOPQRSTUVW
XYZ 1234567890 .,:;"«»ß&!?

Those who have known Dennis over the more than thirty years that he has been making silk purses of what have often been the sow's ears of numerous periodicals are perhaps the only ones who know how much he has influenced the way magazines look in Britain today. It is also astonishing to many of us how he ever manages to get these jobs done when he can easily spend a day considering the best way to assemble the letters that he needs to make three words. It is not astonishing, though, that he was elected a Royal Designer for Industry.

Walbaum

My unqualified favourite. To my mind the best of the 19th century Didot typefaces – particularly for text setting. Most agreeable, it has made the transition from its original letterpress form to film and digital technology without losing any of its crispness and strength. Also, a plus – it hasn't been tampered with, 'improved'. It remains a family of roman, italic and a bold. The italic and the bold have exactly the correct emphasis in relation to the central roman. What more could you want? Well, it also looks terrific when enlarged up for, say on a poster, especially in lower case.

DENNIS BAILEY

match those of the roman (for example, h, m, and n have serifs at the baseline), but it is far from being an electronically sloped roman and has a liveliness of form associated with italics. Its inclined characters are unusual in being slightly wider overall that their related upright forms, and for this reason some combinations of them are a little too open for my taste. Trump Mediaeval can be forgiven for its eccentric italic ampersand – the result, perhaps, of a rash moment of attention seeking on the part of its designer. Less forgivably, its parentheses and brackets look rather similar in smaller sizes. But if you are searching for a typeface that makes a clear distinction between colons and semi-colons, Trump Mediaeval has to be your choice too.

MICHAEL TWYMAN

abcdefghijklmnopqrstuvwxyz
ABCDEFGHIJKLMNOPQRSTUVWXYZ

abcdefghijklmnopqrstuvwxyz
ABCDEFGHIJKLMNOPQRSTUVWXYZ

The first degree course in Typography in Britain was that at the University of Reading, and it was entirely appropriate that it should have been given to Michael Twyman to set it up. He is distinguished as both a scholar and a teacher, but what makes him so agreeable a companion is that if you come to know him because of only one of his skills you are unlikely to discover more than a few of the others until you have known him for many years.
It is a lucky person who runs into him, perhaps in the sunlight outside a hillside café in Umbria, for even in a cafeteria in Stanford there is a twinkle in his eye.

Trump Mediaeval

My choice is Trump Mediaeval because it is a good workhorse type that
deserves to be better known. It is not old enough to have found much of a
place in the history books, and not new enough to have been promoted
strongly in recent publicity battles. However, one of the advantages of its
relative neglect compared with the household names of type design is that so
far it has avoided plagiarism and has spawned few, if any, look-alikes.
It was designed by Georg Trump for the Stuttgart foundry of C E Weber in
the period 1954-60 and is a registered Linotype-Hell type. One of the reasons
why it is so rarely discussed fully in books on type is that it belongs to the
'Crystal Goblet' category: that is, it doesn't immediately proclaim its identity
by coming between the message and its readers. It is a reserved type that has
no interest in forcing itself on people. I do not know whether Allen Hutt ever
used it, but it has some of the qualities of down to earth pragmatism and
common sense I associate with him.
I have included it in my 'best remembered' category not for the quality of its
individual letterforms – though I warm to them in larger sizes – but
principally for its overall effect. It is assured and harmonious visually, and
robust enough to withstand the hazards of production processes and to work
well on different papers .
Now that I am approaching my sixtieth year and suffer – along with millions
of others – by having to take off my glasses and put them on again many times
a day in order to find the least bad reading conditions, I am grateful for any
type that makes my life easier. I feel that Georg Trump – whom I was
fortunate to meet towards the end of his long life – must have understood the
needs of the older reader. Is it significant, I wonder, that he was almost
exactly the age I am now when he began designing Trump Mediaeval?
Those who enjoy categorizing types would describe the curiously named
Trump Mediaeval as an old-face type with strong angled serifs. It has a large
'x' height, which allows for generous internal shapes in its lower-case
characters and makes it particularly effective in small sizes. By contrast, its
capital letters are rather small and fall below the height of ascending
characters; this helps to minimize the spotty effects often seen in text matter
that has many capitals and is useful when designing material that has whole
words picked out in capitals, such as authors names in bibliographies. It has a
sloped roman rather than a truly cursive italic. This is not to everyone's taste,
but has its uses when it is important to minimize the difference between
upright and inclined variants in a text. Most of its inclined character shapes

At the Working Seminar he had just finished the text version of the design. Because coincidence does not really exist, his type was exactly positioned in the field where I was drawing my lines. But this was not all. It disobeyed all of the rules that I had thought to be appropriate for such a sans serif design. It looked so irregular, with each character featuring its own peculiarities. To my eyes it was sparkling with detail in all of its elements. It was one big idiosyncrasy. I showed him my design and told him that I was striving for evenness and harmony by repeating as many forms as possible. Volker explained to me that he was doing exactly the opposite in order to achieve the same goal. This was how I started to get a visual grip on the interaction of readability and legibility, and this is why for me Today Sans Serif is best to be remembered.

ALBERT JAN POOL

abcdefghijklmnopqrstuvwxyz
ABCDEFGHIJKLMNOPQRSTUVWXYZ
1234567890 .,:;''«»

abcdefghijklmnopqrstuvwxyz
ABCDEFGHIJKLMNOPQRSTUVWXYZ
1234567890 .,:;''«»

Albert Jan Pool, like Petr van Blokland and Peter Matthias Noordzij, was, and is, a key member of what we like to think of as the Dutch mafia, the unmistakably bright alumni of Gerrit's classes in Holland. For the past few years he has been digging himself in at Peter Karow's URW in Hamburg, where most of the pioneering work on outline technology was started in response to the needs of the late Walter Brendel.

Today Sans Serif

Ever tried to design a 'humanist sans serif'? No, not like Optima, more like Gill. Only a few have tried and fewer have succeeded. Apart from Eric Gill and Hans Eduard Meyer (Syntax) nobody came up with anything reasonable until 1987. At least this was my view of the world somewhere in the early 80s, as a student at the Royal Academy of Arts in The Hague. I envisioned a sans serif design that would in fact be a Garamond without contrast, and (of course?) have no serifs. I tried the best I could and left out everything that could be seen as an idiosyncrasy. I strongly disliked Eric Gill's circular o, the symmetrical g, and the 'amateurist M' as I called it; I could not get away with the a in Syntax, and Gerrit Noordzij had just taught me that the italics of both designs were in fact hybrid. Could there be a greater challenge? I was amazed when I discovered Frutiger's Frutiger. Somebody else had almost done it! But there was still something to be done; after all he hadn't done a 'proper' italic either… . I kept on drawing, and every time I had photographed my paste-up (the outline fonts for the Mac had yet to be invented) of 'Pa's wijze lynx bezag vroom het fikse aquaduct' (the Dutch version of 'the quick brown fox'), I realised that it would really be difficult to improve on these guys … .

Then summer came. The ATypI Congress and Working Seminar were about to take place. For the first time I met other designers, almost as famous as the aforementioned three, who had obviously been working on similar designs! At the Congress in Kiel Georg Salden unveiled his Polo (half under the table; we had to be quiet because the meeting of the Committee of Manufacturers and Designers was in full session and we were sitting next to Hermann Zapf, who was just teaching all of us a lesson about the illegal copying of fonts). The Working Seminar was held in Hamburg, and there I got to know Bernd Möllenstädt of Berthold, who showed me his almost finished Formata. I decided that I liked this one more than Polo. The g was much better, but why did he attach those serifs to the stems? Should not we try to do without them? After a few days I got to know Volker Küster. I had not really noticed him during the first days of the Seminar, because he could hardly get out of the type department of Scangraphic. Until very late each evening he was busy realizing the previous night's dreams (and nightmares) of Bernd Holthusen, the visionary Managing Director of the Company. I got to know him too, because I joined Scangraphic 18 months later. After Bernd Holthusen left the dream was over, so I finally left for URW. Volker left a bit earlier, leaving the type department to me, but not before realizing his own dream: Today Sans Serif.

abcdefghijklmnopqrstuvwxyz
ABCDEFGHIJKLMNOPQRSTUVWXYZ
1234567890 .,::''«»ß&!?

abcdefghijklmnopqrstuvwxyz
ABCDEFGHIJKLMNOPQRSTUVWXYZ
1234567890 .,::''«»ß&!?

abcdefghijklmnopqrstuvwxyz
ABCDEFGHIJKLMNOPQRSTUVW
XYZ 1234567890 .,::''«»ß&!?

Those who have known Dennis over the more than thirty years that he has been making silk purses of what have often been the sow's ears of numerous periodicals are perhaps the only ones who know how much he has influenced the way magazines look in Britain today. It is also astonishing to many of us how he ever manages to get these jobs done when he can easily spend a day considering the best way to assemble the letters that he needs to make three words. It is not astonishing, though, that he was elected a Royal Designer for Industry.

Three Sans Faces

Sans Serif: Futura, ATF's Franklin Gothic, Standard Medium
Sans Serifs, a clutch of three: Futura the perfect ruler and compass sans.
Regular, Demi-Bold, Extra-Bold — in caps or lower case, all great to use.
Wonderful graphic numerals. ATF's Franklin Gothic (not the 'new' ITC
version) both in Regular and Italic and condensed for editorial and advertising
headlines, works well with other faces; Standard medium (Akzidenz Grotesk
halb-felt, Berthold) the classic grotesque display face.

DENNIS BAILEY

He then reached into a desk and pulled out a gi
ngham check duster. He handed it to me and sai
d: You know, there are over 14,000 books in thi
s library. I want you to dust them all, they collec
t the dust on the tops. So take them out one by

*He then reached into a desk and pulled out a gi
ngham check duster. He handed it to me and s
aid: You know, there are over 14,000 books in
this library. I want you to dust them all, they c
ollect the dust on the tops. So take them out o*

*Max Caflisch is a Swiss book designer and teacher who has never been addicted to
a grid system or to the use of the most mechanical sans serifs. His books are as
carefully crafted as Swiss watches, and he has a way with type ornaments which
adds and light a decorative touch to his bookwork. As typographical advisor to the
firm of Hell, he has been instrumental in bringing many handsome new text types
into existence, and he has in recent years written many carefully researched
reviews of recent text types for the trade press.*
J D

impressed by the high quality of the drawings and said as much at the time. Later I learned that Monotype had declined to buy the design because according to them it was too similar to their Gill Sans. Admittedly Syntax is based on the same principles as Gill, namely that the shape and proportion of the letters follow those of earlier for better legibility. Gill Sans was one of the best horses in the Monotype stables, and around 1960 written letterforms were in increasing demand on the European continent. They obviously wanted to avoid competition to that type face. The next step back is to the origins from which the new typeface was developed in the late 1950s. After years of trying to achieve maximum discipline in a script typeface Meier had the idea of converting the perfection of humanistic script into a sans serif face. After countless attempts this concept finally led to Syntax.

The initiative to develop a new typeface usually starts with discussions based on trial settings, or with ideas on how to improve the form of a typeface to accommodate either a trend or new technical methods of reproduction. In this case the goal was to put up against statically constructed grotesk designs or sans serif linear typefaces a naturally dynamic form based on Renaissance script. Various versions of Syntax, not even called Grotesk, complement each other beautifully and show how well Hans Eduard Meier has succeeded in this task. Today it is one of the best sans serif typefaces. It is so good that companies have copied it and offered it under different names to their customers – Symphony, Synchron, Synthesis – which is, by the way, a highly dubious practice.

If one considers how long it takes to make a typeface from first drawings to a final form which can be offered for sale you can appreciate that a type designer must get used to holding his breath for a long time! The five versions of Syntax Antiqua, and the later typefaces Barbedor and Syndor prove that the designer and calligrapher Hans Eduard Meier, who is both perceptive and capable of detailed work of the utmost subtlety, has got used to doing just that.

MAX CAFLISCH

abcdefghijklmnopqrstuvwxyz
ABCDEFGHIJKLMNOPQRSTUVWXYZ
1234567890.,'':;-()!?£$&fiflffifflflffß

abcdefghijklmnopqrstuvwxyz
ABCDEFGHIJKLMNOPQRSTUVWXYZ
1234567890.,'':;-()!?£$&fiflffifflflffß

Syntax

In the ATypI type directory published in 1975, dates for versions of Syntax Antiqua produced by the Type foundry D Stempel AG in Frankfurt were given as follows: Antiqua 1968, Demibold 1969, Extra Bold 1970, and Bold 1971, Italic 1972. But the actual production of the Syntax family required a substantially longer time to develop.

First proofs of the prototype 10pt Antiqua were dated 2nd and 7th June 1967. A corrected new casting produced carries the date of September 11 1967. In the three months between the first and second set of proofs, every letter had been cast individually on an increased width of between .02 and 0.03mm. The changes in the fit, although very small, were an obvious improvement. Thereafter these changes became the basis for the widths of the other text sizes. They show how subtly the characters were adjusted in order to give maximum legibility to the small sizes – a normal process for a type foundry working to strict quality criteria.

Cutting of the other sizes continued until 30th August 1968.

Neither a layman nor a judge who has to assess on the basis of the software production date whether a typeface has been imitated or illegally copied has any idea of the amount of preliminary work necessary for a typeface to reach this advanced state. Already in May 1965 I had received from the type designer Hans Eduard Meier a black hardboard portfolio containing seven times six pages with the same printed text on them. On each page was one size of the type face in its normal, italic and semibold versions. The text had been produced by pasting every character into position, one by one, and then printing the text to give the appearance of a page in a book. The sizes were from 18 pt down to 6 point, and the italic sizes were in two sets of slightly varying widths. The positioning of each letter was meticulously executed by hand. Because there were pages of every version and size it was possible to assess the appearance of the typeface beforehand, and to make the appropriate corrections in the subsequent production stages in the type foundry. These hand made pages indicated in principle the final shape of the typeface.

Now I will take a step back in the decision process. I remember that in 1960 I had a chance to see the earlier drafts of the typeface. At this time I was often doing work for the Berne office of the Monotype Corporation. In a meeting I was shown drawings made by Meier, together with text set in Garamond by Deberny & Peignot, in order to demonstrate the similarity between the new sans serif and the Renaissance Antiqua in shape and proportion. I was much

ABCDEFGHIJKLMNOPQRSTUVWXYZ&
abcdefghijklmnopqrstuvwxyz 1234567890

ABCDEFGHIJKLMNOPQRSTUVWXYZ&
abcdefghijklmnopqrstuvwxyz 1234567890

Don't try to impress Kathleen with a bad typeface. A mediocre typeface might be forgiven if it were wrapped around the label of a particularly good bottle of wine. Actually, it's difficult to begin a description of Kathleen without resorting immediately to 'typefaces and wine'. After all, where is she usually found? We all meet at odd points on the globe for tradeshows, conferences, and such – but really, mostly for dinner. In real life, she is a prolific author, reporting on and grumbling about electronic typography, publishing, and prepress. One can only assume she does so because the field of reporting on fine cuisine is so crowded. Kathleen once explained to me why she spends so much time with fonts – she said something along the lines of 'I write about prepress issues because it's my livelihood; I hang around this other crowd simply because I so love the type'.

Stellar

It sometimes seems as if every typeface that ever lived has already been revived for the desktop, sometimes regrettably (or forgettably, at least). But there are also faces that ought to be available but aren't, among them many of the serviceable types produced by R H Middleton for Ludlow.

My favorite of these is Stellar. It has legible characters, gently modulated stems, and elegantly flared terminals. Text set in Stellar looks good on the page and makes you want to read it. Like Optima, which has similar details, this face won't fare too well at low resolution, but it would be a wonderful semi-sans for text when the budget supports imagesetter output. I wish some sensitive font-maker would produce Stellar for the desktop.

KATHLEEN TINKEL

But still the John Bull printing kit
Delight our yearning gaze.
And though the Fournier has to go,
And we junk Bodoni Bold,
We'll hold fast the stately types of England.

SEBASTIAN CARTER

ABCDEGHJKMNQRSTUW

abcdefghijklmnopqrstuvwxyz
ABCDEFGHIJKLMNOPQRSTUV
WXYZ 1234567890 .,:;"«»ß&!?

Sebastian Carter combines the craftsmanly gifts of his father Will with the literary and intellectual talents of his uncle John Carter. He broadened his experience by working for a time in Paris with Arnold Fawcus at the Trianon Press, then he worked partly with his father at the Rampart Lions Press in Cambridge, and also as a freelance book designer and writer. He has written books on twentieth century type designers and on the theory of book design, and is a frequent contributor to Matrix. Sebastian conveys a clear impression of independent and astute views, charitably expressed. He continues to operate the Rampart Lions Press from Over, near Cambridge.
J D

Stately Types

To be sung in the bath, to half-remembered snatches of Noel Coward's
Stately Homes of England.

Lord Baskerville, Lord Caslon
Lord Bulmer and Lord Bell –
With every virtue, every grace,
We represent a good type face.

Here you see the pick of us
You may be slightly sick of us,
Still, we're what you really need
In this devoid-of-merit age
To give a sense of heritage,
And while a bit démodé,
An antidote to Brody.

Though we're old, and spiky,
And rather Rogers-and-Updikey
Products of an ancient craft,
We are the remnants of an old
And fine collection
That on reflection
Doesn't seem quite so daft.

The stately types of England,
How well we love them all,
Though if we really have to choose
It's Caslon wall-to-wall.
The Figginses and Thorowgoods
Have all seen better days,
The Aldines and the Garamonds
Are just a passing craze,
Times and Palatino
Hold temporary sways,

abcdefghijklmnopqrstuvwxyz
ABCDEFGHIJKLMNOPQRSTUVW
XYZ 1234567890 .,:;''«»ß&!?

abcdefghijklmnopqrstuvwxyz
ABCDEFGHIJKLMNOPQRSTUVW
XYZ 1234567890 .,:;''«»ß&!?

The task of coming to ITC after Aaron Burns is one that few would relish. ITC was always Aaron's company from the days when he first arrived in Bruges with Julius Bloom (was that really his name, or do I forget?) and Ed Gottschall. They came to make their presentations to the type founders gathered there. It cannot be easy to come to a company to replace somebody whom everybody loves.
One of the many reasons that his friends like Mark Batty is his courage and loyalty. But more than that is that he has absolutely no image of himself as an important person, a quality which those of us who find it sometimes difficult to be made fun of envy most dreadfully.

Souvenir

If Gilbert and Sullivan had been around today, and had they had their attention focused on the USA, they may well have been writing of 'the very model of an American Typeface'.

That typeface is ITC Souvenir.

ITC Souvenir is Broadway rather than Carnegie Hall, Chevrolet rather than Mercedes, ribs rather than sushi.

In fact, as it turns out, ITC Souvenir has been the very embodiment and representation of the most catholic zeitgeist of the middle 1970s onwards.

And it is a quintessentially American typeface, with real solid character. The typeface somehow communicates optimism, it is friendly, wholesome, and undemanding to the eye.

ITC Souvenir could not be described as particularly elegant or sophisticated, but not all jobs need these traits. In fact, most do not, and this is a reason the typeface can be constantly seen in virtually all applications ranging from corporate work, advertising, magazines, stuff like menus, through to correspondence.

So what has made ITC Souvenir one of the top ten most successful ITC typefaces of all time?

Soft edges and round corners work well at a wide variety of sizes and on most printing surfaces, making the typeface widely usable. A large x-height and open counters make the typeface highly legible and readable. The typeface has a strong differentiating personality. In short, it has the qualities to make it a great little communicator.

ITC Souvenir is not fashion or fad or style, and is never the subject of polite dinner conversation anywhere. Talk to designers at random, and they will deny using it, ever. But look around, and you will see it everywhere.

Whatever anyone says, this makes ITC Souvenir one of a handful of the greatest typefaces of all time. To say otherwise is just posturing.

MARK BATTY

correspondence and as my on-screen typing face. In print I tend to use more classically beautiful faces such as Bembo, Bodoni, Bernhard anything, ITC Berkeley OldStyle, Cheltenham, Electra, Galliard, Goudy Old Style, Gill Sans, Kabel, Weiss, and as many display faces I can get my hands on, with my latest favorites being Emigre's Remedy, Carter & Cone's Mantinia, and LetterPerfect's Spumoni. I'm also working with Jason Castle to revive some wonderful faces Gustav Jensen designed in the '20s.

Hmm... When it comes right down to it, I guess Serifa is who I really am (at least for the moment) – but Galliard is still who I want to be.

DANIEL WILL-HARRIS

abcdefghijklmnopqrstuvwxyz
ABCDEFGHIJKLMNOPQRSTUVWXYZ
1234567890 .,:;''«»ß&!?

abcdefghijklmnopqrstuvwxyz
ABCDEFGHIJKLMNOPQRSTUVWXYZ
1234567890 .,:;''«»ß&!?

If there is a more prolific writer on desk-top publishing in the United States than Daniel Will-Harris, it could only be because somebody else is writing under two different names. Not only will you find many of his books in every bookshop, but there will also be few weeks where you won't also find an article of his in one of the many journals which cater to the need we all have of wanting to find out how to use more of the tools that we buy.

Serifa's just my type

I say that 'a typeface is your personality on paper'. You know how people's pets often look like them? The same applies to a person's choice of typeface. That's why I was originally reluctant to write about Serifa. I like of think of myself as the 'Bernhard Modern' type, while I'm probably more the 'Bernhard Bold Condensed' type.

So I'm not sure where Serifa fits into my personality, except that it's a workaholic. A few years ago I would have called you crazy if you'd told me that I'd be singing the praises of Serifa. That's because a few years ago I didn't like Serifa. I thought it looked like typewriter type and I was too enamoured with beautiful faces such as Galliard or Goudy Old Style to actually see Serifa.

Then one day I saw Serifa in print – it made a real impression because I still remember what it was – the instruction manual for the Z88, Sir Clive's one pound Scottish computer. The typeface looked simultaneously modern, mechanical, 'Europeanish,' and even kind of cute. I'm a sucker for cute.

I started to use it for my personal correspondence because so much of it was going out via fax instead of mail and Serifa looks very good, even after faxing. It grew on me, and now what once looked kind of 'klunky' to me now has considerable hardworking charm.

I should explain why I prefer Serifa to Rockwell, Glypha, or Memphis, three typefaces that most people would find as nearly identical as they find Helvetica and Univers (Univers being preferable of course, if for no other reason than it works perfectly with Serifa – since Serifa is after all a slab-serifed Univers).

Rockwell looks somehow old fashioned and uneven (the lowercase a is ugly and if you don't like a typeface's a you'd better not use it). Memphis looks like Futura with slab serifs and I find it very hard to read. Glypha was designed by Frutiger nine years after Serifa. To me it looks like Serifa after a 'large x-height' once-over – which was one too many as far as I'm concerned — it's too condensed and too bland.

And just because I like Serifa doesn't mean I've stopped looking. Lately I've been flirting with other slab serif faces – PMN Caecilia is softer, quirkier, has old style figures, gen-u-ine italics (something Serifa regrettably lacks), and is condensed without looking condensed, so it fits more type on a page. It seems more personal, but it lacks Serifa's sharp, open look.

I should also make one more thing clear: only once have I used Serifa as the typeface for a book: a book about typing. Other than that I only use it for

THE QUICK BROWN FOX JUMPS 4

THE QUICK BROWN

ABCDEFGHIJKLMNOPQRSTUVWXYZ
ÆŒ& 1234567890£ ,.:;-'

Until he abandoned everything to breed hedgehogs in Norfolk, David Deadman
had a distinguished design career, first with Banks & Miles and then in
partnership with Peter Stone, who is much missed. There are few people in Britain
who have not seen some examples of his fine work.
But he also has a very bad memory. The letterhead that he designed at Banks
and Miles for Photoscript used Sans Serifs Shaded.

Sans Serif Shaded

When I was a student I was seduced by Sans Serif Shaded.

We were given a wonderful book of Type Specimens by Stephenson Blake, the Caslon Letter Foundry, Sheffield, which showed about 200 faces all displayed in those never to be forgotten words 'The quick brown fox jumps over the lazy dog', which in case you don't know contain every letter of the alphabet.

In those days we had to trace letters out of the book for our layouts and it was always a problem because the specimen of 48 pt might show only the words 'Big Brown' and they were never the letters you wanted, so we were forced to draw, which was no bad thing.

There were treasures such as Baskerville Old Face and Caslon in their original form, together with beauties like Thorowgood Italic, Thorne Shaded or Old Face Open.

But for some reason Sans Serif Shaded took my fancy then – and it still does. It shouts of Steam Engines and the Industrial Revolution – the sort of lettering you cast in brass or paint on a locomotive in brown and cream.

I've wanted to use it for 35 years. I've done pencil roughs using it and even finished visuals but never a printed specimen. I seem to remember it being used successfully in Architectural Review and I think I know how to use it when the time comes.

Best forgotten? Never, one day my chance will come.

DAVID DEADMAN

```
1 2 3 4 5 6 7 8 9 0 ½ =
q w e r t y u i o p - [
  a s d f g h j k l ; ] ⅜
> z x c v b n m , . ½
```

To follow in the footsteps of Bror Zachrisson as head of the Graphic Institute in Stockholm is a job I wouldn't have wished on a cat. Chris Ottander has managed to make his own climate without ever earning anything but the admiration of those of us who were close to Bror. But there is a serious difference in approach. Where with Bror it was golf, with Chris, as befits a Swede, it is boats.

Prestige Elite

The typeface most often forgotten and remembered with hate/love is the one appearing in typewritten text – Remington, Underwood, Adler, Halda, Façit – everyone you could name used it.

The typeface was named Elite. Designed to be distributed in mimeographs and Gigher-duplicators. Ugly even in original. But forever tied to knowledge in school examination papers. Thesis manuscripts. The original text. The typeface closest to thought. Your own thoughts and those of your tutors. Elite – the name is congenial.

The original typeface for my generation need not be aesthetic, beautiful or legible because reading in the beginning is hard, dull and difficult and knowledge is hidden behind, beyond the letters.

The distortions of the mimeographed versions added to the challenge of reading and attempts to understand.

Ugliness prevails over beauty.

CHRIS OTTANDER

ABCDEFGHIJKLMNOP
abcdefghijkm nopqrstuvwyz
1234567890
ABCDEFGHIJKLMNOPQ
abcdefghijklmnopqrstuvwyz
1234567890

People march to different drums. Few had the good fortune to find a drum that brought them a small design studio in Gig Harbor in the State of Washington, where they could be paid both to design graphics and make fonts.
It must have taken some heavy bribery to get him to leave, even to an office so well placed overlooking Puget Sound as that of Elseware. Here he now helps them with their elastic fonts, that newest and perhaps most frightening of the options that the computer has brought to type manufacture.

Preissig

I know nothing of Vojtech Preissig, except for this marvelously idiosyncratic typeface which he left us from his commission with the Czechoslovakian Printing Office in Prague, published by Grafotechna in 1929. 'Tortured, quirky, comic' – these are all qualities that the face evokes, yet even at text settings, it is remarkably readable. The overall impression of its jaggedness, which is mainly evidenced in the curves, is effectively reconciled and anchored by the straight and regular vertical stems and serifs. All this is to say that Vojtech has either luckily, or purposefully, pulled off the challenge of a functional, deconstructed roman typeface – a predecessor to the 'random fonts' of the digital era. Recently I cracked open a book of Czech poetry which was set in this esoteric face. Though I couldn't read the poesy, Preissig delighted me with its own jaunty dance across and down the page. The message was sure to be clever and friendly – or inexorably made more so. (The italic pushes this envelope further, achieving greater quirkiness and compromised legibility.)

GARRETT BOGE

SYRACVSE ROME

Corps Quarante-Huit.

CINQVIEMES

Ladislas Mandel worked with Charles Peignot at Deberny & Peignot during the period of the development of the Lumitype – which became the Photon in America – and the period when Adrian Frutiger was also there. His great interest in the working of mechanical and electronic machines complemented his fine eye for type. Those of us who have never been able to kick the ATypI habit fondly hold numerous memories of his slight corduroy-suited figure among the French contingent. We also remember that he shares with the editor (and Max and Mike?) a reluctance to use one word when six will do.

which was easier on the reader's eye and more to his taste, in other words a more readable type to make the text more intelligible. By reviving types of an earlier period classified now by the name Garaldes (an amalgam of the name of Garamond the punchcutter and Aldus the publisher-patron of new types in the fifteenth century) Perrin deliberately abandoned Didot's principles. His typeface was closer to Garamond than to Jenson, but the shapes of his letters are more versatile, have more rhythm and are slightly rounder. He gave his letters a dynamic and oblique angle of stress, he fitted them more loosely; he made the ascenders and descenders almost twice as tall as the x-height. Nevertheless they look extremely elegant and sober, and they combine precision with fluency.

He brought about a rebirth of the art of text typography for continuous reading by returning to the great tradition of French typography created by Garamond, Granjon, Jannon, Luce and Fournier. This typographical revival of Louis Perrin's brought back a taste for Old Face types by Beaudoire and others. However this movement was not entirely fortuitous, for above all it met new social demands on printing from a new section of the reading public. For however much expanding industries needed qualified workmen for the success of its products, the press (with many daily newspapers) needed a typographical dress which would make for easy reading. However, through typography getting its second wind by rediscovering historical values, the way was opened up for the real democratization of written communication – the key to knowledge and learning. So the rehabilitation of decent letterforms for bookwork in modern times thoroughly merits showing our gratitude to the modest initiatives of Louis Perrin's work as a typographer.

LADISLAS MANDEL

[1] In his preface to Louis Perrin's exhibition catalogue, Lyon 1923.
[2] Louis Perrin

CARACTERES AVGVSTAVX

HONNEVR

Corps Soixante-Douze.

ANCIEN

Louis Perrin typefaces

The movement led by Fournier le Jeune in the mid-18th century to combat a general lowering of typographical standards, as well as the frigid formality of the Romain du Roi types, lasted only a short time. The royal types were later given a further spell of popularity during the Empire years by the last of the Didot types, which appeared while painting was under David's severe neo-classical influence.

In these icy domineering types, stiffness almost stifled feeling. Heavy and static verticals were in stark contrast with extremely fragile horizontal lines, and outweighed the sensuous curves in the letters. All this created a sort of static screen over the lifeless page and caused eye fatigue to the reader.

The French Revolution was more interested in citizens' education than with teaching or culture: typography was utterly ignored. Eventually a lead was taken by emerging industrial power. However it had nothing to do with the spread of ideas through books, or with improving the lot of the reading public. Industry's concern was with publicity by enlisting typography to create a visual shock. Thus display types came into existence.

This led Marius Audin to observe:[1]

'For the past fifty years (he wrote in 1850) printers have been in bondage to Didot and his dogmas. But one man at least was deeply upset to see great traditions pass into oblivion: he tried desperately to fight against this denial of what was right. He suffered from having to use these styles of type in his daily work; he recognized that they had been struck with such accuracy, cast and aligned so evenly and displaying such mathematical symmetry. He saw their merits but wanted to restrict their use to printing reports on the railways.'

About 1846, Louis Perrin, a Lyonnais printer and a keen archaeologist described by Audin as 'the best typographer', had a set of 'Augustales' capitals engraved for use in his edition of De Boissieu's *Inscriptions Antiques de Lyon*. As he found Didot's capitals unsuitable for this work, he took the inspiration for his Augustales capitals from classical letterforms cut in stone in Lyon. A short time afterwards he came across some long-neglected sixteenth century types in Monsieur Rey's workshop, and these looked perfect to Perrin. They gave him the idea of going back to livelier Renaissance letterforms and instilled in him a taste for the sixteenth century whose greatest achievements seemed to Perrin never to have been surpassed. For use with his 'Augustales' capitals, he accordingly designed lower case letters which were engraved by Fougère and cast by Rey. Perrin wanted to create perfect harmony between typeface and text. And flying in the face of fashion, he wanted a typeface

ABCDEFGHIJKLMNOPQRSTUVWXYZÆŒ&

abcdefghijklmnopqrstuvwxyz

1234567890

All sorts of people have come and gone from the Linotype subsidiary at Cheltenham. Cheltenham has had periods when they were pulling in money as though it was free, and there were also times when perhaps the company was suffering from having threatened the role of subsidiaries in other countries. Through all these years we have all sat, from time to time, near the slightly hunched figure of Alan Shelley, at one of those committee meetings that form so large a part of our working lives.

There are few of us on the circuit who do not hold fond memories of his thoughtful rustic voice, and wise words.

Pegasus

Perhaps I could add a paragraph of admiration for Berthold Wolpe's Pegasus, a much unsung typeface. This fine typeface has been much under publicised and under used. It was applied to great effect back in 1980, by MF Graphics of Saffron Walden, when using VIP film fonts especially prepared by Matthew Carter, to set the V&A 'retrospective' catalogue of Wolpe's work. While his Albatross typeface has received universal acclaim and is widely used (and copied) the Pegasus face never really got its just reviews.

It was Stanley Morison who invited Wolpe to 'design a book type' – which he promptly did, astonishingly, in only three months. The numerals he cut later. The design of Pegasus is almost unique in that when he produced the face back in 1938 it was/is such that it could be enlarged or reduced without any distortion. Perhaps the most incredible of undertakings was that Wolpe drew the whole alphabet in 12 pt, so precisely, that no changes were necessary by the type founders.

I am no longer in the business of promoting type, but I feel this is a very good typeface which has been much overlooked.

You may recall Berthold constantly grumbling about his underpaid commission (he even raised it at the Double Crown Club). He was quite convinced, wrongly, that Pegasus was being sold in large numbers. It was mostly his mates who had the face.

ALAN SHELLEY

abcdefghijklmnopqrstuvwxyz
ABCDEFGHIJKLMNOPQRSTUVWXYZ
1234567890 .,:;"«»ß&!?

abcdefghijklmnopqrstuvwxyz
ABCDEFGHIJKLMNOPQRSTUVWXYZ
1234567890 .,:;"«»ß&!?

If you need to know something about the graphic industry, there are conventional
ways of solving the problem. You can go to libraries. You can subscribe to trade
magazines. You can visit shows. You can do all of these things. But if you would
rather spend time on the beach you need do none of these things.
You just ask Colin Cohen.

Palatino

Palatino – probably the best typeface in the world. Designed to a rigorous, pre-DTP, specification to withstand not only the rigours of newspaper printing by letterpress and litho, but also for output on a number of different hot metal manufacturers' equipment in the days before type was device independent.

Despite this it is more than serviceable for both text and display, has a good italic but lacks an extra bold.

As a result of its origins it can withstand any reprographic process with dignity – even a 300 dpi laser printer and poor photocopying

After Palatino there was little need for any new faces but …

COLIN COHEN

abcdefghijklm
nopqrstuvwxyz
ABCDEFGHIJK
LMNOPQRSTU
VWXYZ
& 12345 SMALL
CAPS 67890

abcdefghijklm
nopqrstuvwxyz
& 1234567890
ABCDEFGHIJKL
MNOPQRSTUV
WXYZ

It is risky to say anything about this man. His thoughts are always original. His design is always his own. His teaching has been exceptional, and his students are now beginning to overrun Europe, and perhaps the best thing they have learned from him is never to think in clichés.

But it is wise to have a place near the door if you have been silly enough to make a foolish or provocative statement in his hearing.

Otherwise you may never hear the last of it.

Noordzij Bible

The efforts of finding the compromise can now be turned to devising the ideal match of script and task. This typeface has grown up in a few editions of the Bible. The Bible could be an average book if one volume would not contain more than an average of one million characters. In common typography the Bible would occupy 6 or 7 volumes. Yet it is also common to demand this vast corpus of Semitic literature in one single volume. For the reader's convenience in 1572 the French printer Robert Estienne had introduced numbered verse and references. An average of 150 numerals on a page, more than in a financial report, demands the integration of numerals in the typeface. This condition alone reduces the options to a very small number of typefaces. This particular typeface has done its duty decently. I have even discovered its qualities for other jobs with narrow measures. I am still contemplating with wonder the small line feel that this composition requires.

GERRIT NOORDZIJ

RONton

RONton

Eiichi is unique in many ways. He is kinder and more courteous and more patient
than any of us. But he also stands alone as a bridge between graphics in Japan
and graphics in Europe and America. Having studied at the London College of
Printing, and taken a post graduate degree at the Royal College of Art in London
he continued his thorough grounding by working in various design studios in
England. For example, he did most of the work of preparing the variation of
Matthew Carter's Bell Centennial that was used for the phone books in England.
But he has designed Latin alphabets for Japanese foundries, and helped with the
preparation of kanji and kana alphabets for Western foundries.
Everybody lucky enough to know him tends to need him for one reason or another,
if only his impeccable eye, and his unfailing good manners.

New Helvetica

MacDonald's has always been busy and Helvetica has been seen everywhere in the world. I once loved the taste of the Mac, which I had acquired on the way back from school in Tokyo long ago, and I adored the typeface until I developed a more sophisticated typographic palate at the London College of Printing in the mid 70's. (If a Big Mac is regarded as a low resolution font, LCP's canteen food was worse than distorted bitmap fonts). Just as I still occasionally eat that awful hamburger without discomfort, I am obliged to overdose on the typeface to satisfy demands, mainly from my innocent Japanese clients. Helvetica (and Century Schoolbook as a representative serif) are almost standard European character sets bundled with Japanese fonts, so they feel very comfortable with Helvetica. I could not tell myself whether I loved it or hated it, but I had been somehow embarrassed to even contemplate using it. And then several years ago I came across a new name, 'Neue Helvetica' listed with the old 'Helvetica' in a Linotype catalogue, and I just dismissed it as the same old bore. Only recently by chance I set a text in the new Hell with my Mac (this is a computer). How refreshing! It looked softer, clearer and less obtrusive, but retained all the good characteristics of the old Hell. Thanks to Mac, a very detailed study on a PostScript typeface (whatever it means) is now possible for anyone who uses Mac or PC with Windows for TrueType (whatever it means, again), and I did it too. There are many subtle but distinctive differences between the new and old Hells which contribute to their individually unique texture, colour, spatial effect and legibility. The new Hell's lower lowercase sets wider than the old one and is more rounded, which seems to contribute to better legibility in smaller sizes. The strokes are more even, the corners are sharper and the counters are slightly wider overall compared with the old one. It was a great moment when I felt myself finally liberated from my dreadfully cleaving Hell-guilt complex. I said to myself unhesitatingly, 'I relish the new Helvetica and the old one too'. Having made an important discovery for the rest of my typographic career, I felt much indebted to LCP's hard training (for the first time ... I guess).

EIICHI KONO

abcdefghijklmnopqrstuvwxyz
ABCDEFGHIJKLMNOPQRSTUVW
XYZ 1234567890 ..:;"«»β&!?

abcdefghijklmnopqrstuvwxyz
ABCDEFGHIJKLMNOPQRST
UVWXYZ 1234567890 ..:;"«»β&!?

The United States is a great country for trade associations. Trade associations need people willing to give time, thought and effort for little visible reward, and America seems to have more people like this. But it is probably true to say that to any US typesetter or typefounder the modest Charles Mulliken's name will be better known than almost any in this book.

Murray Hill & Murray Hill Bold

How could anybody forget Murray Hill or Murray Hill Bold? Half the florist delivery trucks and fashion signage in North America use the Murray Hill style of lettering. The typeface was designed as a metal type for American Typefounders in 1956 by Emil J Klump, a famous handlettering artist turned type designer. Mr Klump was paid .05¢ a pound royalty for 20 years. Had he been paid .000005¢ per sign for a year, he would be a rich man today.

CHARLES W MULLIKEN

ABCDEFG?
HKLMOPQ
123456789

Of all the Stephensons and all the Blakes who have steered this famous old type foundry through good times and bad, acquiring other companies in good times, and preserving what they have in bad, few have drawn a shorter straw than Charles. He was given the reins as digital typesetting drove a few more nails into the coffin of hand set metal, and has successfully held them through all the misfortunes that have fallen upon so many heavy industries in most parts of the world. These are the industries that were the heart of Sheffield which also reflected Stephenson Blake's many interests.

They used to say that even the sparrows cough in Sheffield. That is why, perhaps, people in that part of the world are so good at surviving.

Molé Foliate

During my early days at the S.B Type Foundry in Sheffield I worked in the Departments involved in punch cutting, engraving and the justification of matrices. A fascinating experience being with craftsmen and using the old gauges, measuring devices and other tools of the trade.

In the late 1950's S.B got permission from Joh. Enschede to reproduce one of their faces, Molé Foliate, on the Anglo American Point System. I was personally involved in the production of the matrices and the problems of converting from the Didot measurement. The reason that this Face is best remembered by me is because of the happy memories of my first visit to Enschede in Haarlem and meeting Mr S L Hartz with whom I stayed, and meeting members of the Enschede family.

It is a marvellous decorative face and among others was used successfully by S.B on some of their own publicity material. On an historical note, Molé invented hollow metal furniture, which he patented in 1815. He was a Punch Cutter and Type Founder and worked in close contact with P Didot l'Aîné who printed for him, and of course Enschedé dealt with him as well.

CHARLES STEPHENSON

abcdefghijklmnopqrstuvwxyz
ABCDEFGHIJKLMNOPQRSTUVWXYZ
1234567890 1234567890 .,:;''«»ß&!?

abcdefghijklmnopqrstuvwxyz
ABCDEFGHIJKLMNOPQRSTUVWXYZ
1234567890 1234567890 .,:;''«»ß&!?

*Matthew Carter inherited from his father Harry a taste for typographical history
and a talent for type-cutting and type design. After working freelance in London
during the swinging sixties, having learnt punchcutting in Harlem at Enschedeen
en Zonen, he was hired by Mergenthaler Linotype in Brooklyn to draw types.
Later he created the firm of Bitstream in Cambridge, Mass. with Mike Parker.
Best known for his design of Galliard, he is a lanky, lucid and influential figure
upon the typographical scene to which he contributes a great deal in design and
dogma.
J D*

Meridian

A poster typeset in Meridian hangs opposite the chair in my dentist's office. Aversion therapy repeated over many visits has failed to break me of my feelings for this face. This can be no ordinary love. I put it down to the following: Meridian was Adrian Frutiger's first text type and exciting as the first evidence of his genius.

Frutiger's explanation for the structural basis of its letterforms (that the triangular serifs make simple negative shapes within and between letters) is one of very few explanations of a typeface by its designer that is at all convincing or interesting. Ordinarily, the more logical the rationale the more post-rationalized it sounds.

It has a semi-bold – which in most type families means half-assed – that is not only good but better even than the regular roman. It has a texture of its own, something to do with the contrast between rich strokes and sharp serifs. If you see a page at a distance and can identify the typeface before you can read the words you are looking at a great typeface. This is possible for me with Meridian Semi-Bold and not a great many others.

It has a beautiful name. I am conditioned to like it: having lived on longitude 0° I have a Greenwichocentric fondness for the meridian. And to an Englishman, of course, the word suggests 'meridional' and the noonday sun.

MATTHEW CARTER

It was certainly a wonderful tribute to Bill Garth, to have a typeface named after him, especially such a grand and expansive family. But I think it is a wonderful tribute and memorial to John Matt, who created the designs, to have one of his designs named after him, Matt Antique, with the same design the basis for the tribute to Bill Garth, with a face named Garth Graphic.

BILL WHEATLEY

abcdefghijklmnopqrstuvwxyz
ABCDEFGHIJKLMNOPQRSTUVWXYZ
1234567890 .,:;''«»ß&!?

abcdefghijklmnopqrstuvwxyz
ABCDEFGHIJKLMNOPQRSTUVWXYZ
1234567890 .,:;''«»ß&!?

They say that the Atlantic has shrunk. But despite this there has been remarkably little communication between the graphic world in the United States and that in the rest of the world. Names that are well-known in America may be unknown elsewhere, though this is not as likely as the fact that names that are well known elsewhere are entirely unknown in the USA. In one direction there are exceptions like Zapf and Frutiger. In the other direction perhaps Bill Wheatley has done as much as anybody to acquaint Europe with how America thinks, because he lived and worked there long enough, looking after the font needs of several well-known companies, to become part of the scene.

Matt Antique

The typeface that I would like to talk about is a face called Matt Antique by some, and Garth Graphic by others. The creator of both these faces was a very gentle man named John Matt. His last position in the type world was with Triple-I, where he ended his life by going to cancer treatment 3 days a week, until it consumed him, and took his life.

His typeface with different names is a curious and interesting story, and one that I would like to see in print, so others can remember the man, and also have some appreciation of how typefaces used to be created.

The basis for both these typefaces was a design drawn by John Matt, when he was a type designer working at ATF, in Elizabeth, New Jersey. The designs were meant for a machine called the ATF B, which was an eighteen unit second generation typesetter. This machine did not have that long a life, and the machine was discontinued before this type face was released.

Drawings of the roman, italic and bold were kicking around the offices of ATF, and came to the attention of Art Directors at two companies. These companies were Itek, Inc., and Compugraphic. John Schappler, the Art Director at Itek, talked to John Matt about the face, and got permission to use his name for the typeface. Since the face was only in the drawing stage, the design staff at Itek had to draw additional characters, as well as refitting them as they were based on an eighteen unit system, and could be broadened for use on the Itek Quadritek, a low cost second generation typesetter. The result was a three face family of roman, italic and bold, called Matt Antique.

At Compugraphic, a slightly larger project was planned. Compugraphic was looking for a typeface which could be named after Bill Garth, the co-founder of Compugraphic Corp., and a pioneer in the typesetting industry. They wanted a typeface of solid quality, and a typeface that would be a fitting tribute to a man – Bill Garth. They started with the same drawings that Itek used, except since this was to be a grand tribute, they created a major family by using URW's Ikarus System. The end result was a major family consisting of roman, italic and bold, as well as a bold italic, an extra bold, and a condensed and bold condensed. They also created small caps, ligatures, old style figures, as well as a full accent complement for all the major European languages.

abcdefghijklmnopqrstuvwxyz
ABCDEFGHIJKLMNOPQRSTUVWXYZ
1234567890 .,:;''«»ß&!?

abcdefghijklmnopqrstuvwxyz
ABCDEFGHIJKLMNOPQRSTUVWXYZ
1234567890 .,:;''«»ß&!?

If there is anybody in the US who has done more to maintain and preserve standards in letterpress printing than Jack Stauffacher it is probably only Jack Stauffacher who'd think of naming a contender. And he would suggest lots of names simply because he rates himself less highly than we do, and must also know everybody who has any pretensions in that direction. There are a great many people who take the trouble to sit at his feet and gather up such crumbs as may fall from his table. If, as a result of this, he has a great many friends we are all people who guard his friendship jealously. I can think of nothing more important to say about him.

Kis Janson

I have used a 17th century baroque typeface designed by the Hungarian, Nicholas Kis*, for over forty years in all possible typographic styles. This is my favourite.

JACK W STAUFFACHER

*wrongly attributed to Anton Janson

abcdefghijklmnopqrstuvwxyz

ABCDEFGHIJKLMNOPQRSTUVWXYZ

1234567890 .,:;''«»ß&!?

abcdefghijklmnopqrstuvwxyz

ABCDEFGHIJKLMNOPQRSTUVWXYZ

1234567890 .,:;''«»ß&!?

Those who have known Dennis over the more than thirty years that he has been making silk purses of what have often been the sow's ears of numerous periodicals are perhaps the only ones who know how much he has influenced the way magazines look in Britain today. It is also astonishing to many of us how he ever manages to get these jobs done when he can easily spend a day considering the best way to assemble the letters that he needs to make three words. It is not astonishing, though, that he was elected a Royal Designer for Industry.

Kis Janson

A good elegant and very legible typeface. Has adapted well to current setting technology. Berthold's and Monotype's are probably the best versions.

DENNIS BAILEY

abcdefghijklmnopqr
stuvwxyz fiflß&
ABCDEFGHIJKLMN
OPQRSTUVWXYZ

It is difficult to know what we should think of Chuck Bigelow. There are those who think of him as a teacher. Certainly the West Coast of the United States is thickly inlaid with many of his ex-students busily shaping the way that California is going to influence type and graphic design. He is a born teacher, with an immense memory that makes it easy for him to draw on examples to illustrate his points. He may think of himself as a type designer. Certainly the Lucida family, which grows like Topsy, is very close to his heart.

I think of both him and Kris Holmes as prisoners in a rose nursery. Pots used to be as far as the eye could see, wherever there was a flat space in reach of the garden hose. Now, in their new house, the eye can see nearly as far as Japan, and the pots have reverted to scale.

Icone

Among the many typefaces that are worthy of favorable mention is Icone, designed by Adrian Frutiger and released by Linotype in 1980. Icone 45 and 46, the light weights of roman and italic, are especially charming. In the Linotype catalogue, Icone is classed with the 'decorative and display' faces, what the French call 'caractères de fantaisie', but I feel this is a mistake. Icone needs another and better category, as it is a post-modern text face with a surprising medieval accent. The horizontal, bracketed treatment of the beginnings and endings of stems reminds me of the Uncial scripts in which the broad-edged pen angle is horizontal, and the resulting character shapes are open and round. In particular, there is a hint of the Irish Insular half-uncial. However, in Icone, the tips of the stems are flared and the middles of the strokes thinned, in an exaggerated reverse entasis. This produces a texture very different from that of Uncial, more reminiscent of the earlier Rustic style in which a vertically angled broad-edged pen was used to produce letterforms with strong terminals serifs and delicate tapering stems. When I asked him about the scribal antecedents of the face, Frutiger said that he had actually been inspired by an early gothic hand, written with a steep pen angle that similarly combined heavy terminals with light strokes. Whatever the historical antecedents, Frutiger does not copy them directly in Icone, but recreates certain of their visual effects in combination with the sophisticated modern letter forms that he is so skilled at rendering. The result is a subtle but fascinating typographic texture: a darker stipple effect along the base-line and x-line, with a lighter, almost geometric alphabet running in between. Bruno Pfäffli has used Icone very tastefully and effectively as both text and display type in art catalogs and posters for various French museums, and it is a joy to see what it can do in his hands, but I have never seen it used with such a sure touch in America. It is still waiting to be discovered by American typographers.

CHUCK BIGELOW

Q W E R T Y U I O P

q w e r t y u i o p

Jeff Level sees himself as a schizophrenic. Half his life has been pulled towards type. Half his mind is still being pulled towards wine. His knowledge on both subjects is immense. But what he probably won't acknowledge is the fact that his eye may be better than that of anybody contributing to this book. It takes a special skill to know within thousandths of an inch on a drawing three or four inches high that there is a mistake in the drawing that must be corrected if that letter is to be part of an alphabet whose other drawings are on separate pieces of paper. Now that so many typefaces are made on the resolution of a television screen this may be a skill that will disappear.

IBM Script 12-Pitch

Jeff, are you kidding? IBM Script 12-Pitch? A monospaced typewriter face?!
(That reminds me, you can never find an interrobang when you need one, can
you?... which reminds me that the interrobang is probably the only thing
worth remembering about Americana [except for the other thing].)
I have long admired this IBM Script 12-Pitch and two other typewriter faces –
Delegate & Adjutant* designed by John Schappler for IBM in the early '60s.
To me, they represent three notable examples of the triumph of creativity over
the strictures of technology and the ethos of the mundane (I mean, the
Courier, Letter Gothic, Prestige schtick and, the Excelsior, Corona schtick;
you know ... the kind of type design espoused by the SchtickSchrift Atelier).
There is no other monospaced typewriter face that I am aware of quite like
this IBM Script 12-Pitch. It has life, spontaneity and charm (wit?); a fresh
style; a sense of movement. Look at it! Each letter has a kinetic kick; why it's
a slap-in-the-face schtick! It reminds of some of the things Dwiggins said
about Electra – '... electricity, sparks, energy ... warm ... full of blood and
personality ... jump right at you.'
I like this IBM Script 12-Pitch. I like it very much! I admire it. I will always
remember it fondly.

JEFF LEVEL

*If you, gentle reader, are an ATypI member, you may recall that all of your
correspondence from Frau Jung was formerly typewritten in one of those little
monospaced gems...

A little later Lludd had the length and breadth of the island measured and found its centre to be in Oxford. There he had a pit dug, and in the pit he set a vat of the *best mead that could be made, with a silk sheet over the vat, and he himself watched that night and saw the dragons fighting.* When they were tired and worn out they sank onto the sheet and dragged it down to the bottom of the vat, where they drank up the mead and fell

There are probably some people who remember Mike Parker from before he went to Linotype. To the rest of us he was Linotype and Bitstream, and very visible. He has now gravitated to the ideal climate of San Diego and acquired a better half as far diagonally from him as you can get in the United States, tucked away in the northern reaches of New England.

It is pleasant to be reminded that Mike was a scholar before he was a type founder, and it is also pleasant to be reminded that Edouard Hoffmann is as worthy to be credited with Helvetica (and Haas Clarendon and Anzeigen Grotesk) as Stanley Morison is to be with Times New Roman. In fact, if we look at the evidence now coming out of Lanston Monotype archives, perhaps he deserves it rather more.

But then he must also share the blame.

core demanded and received special attention.

I searched for a sans serif design of Swiss character that would meet our specifics for a broad series. It should provide the basis for a central core of strongest possible design. Italics must be moderately sloped, with slope to vary as required by fitting problems in each width and weight. Design features must vary as necessary in peripheral versions. I quietly looked at a number of designs for inspiration, particularly Airport, newly designed for Heathrow by Matthew Carter.

I discovered that Edouard Hoffmann at the Haas type foundry, a distant subsidiary, had produced a magnificent design with the required characteristics, the Haas Grotesk. It lacked only adaptation to the Linotype, and perhaps a new name. Walter Kunz at Stempel, our principal European foundry, was interested in producing a Linotype series, and commissioned the design from Haas. After due consideration, he telephoned Hoffmann and told him that Stempel and Linotype had decided to call the resulting series Helvetica. 'You can't do that' said Hoffmann in horror, 'that's the name of the country.' Five weeks later he returned the call, quietly asking permission to use the new name in Switzerland.

A little later, Jackson Burke called me into the big office to tell me that he had decided to retire within the year, and that I was in line for the job. He told me that Trade Gothic was being finished. To my astonishment, he asked if there was any new design that I felt was important enough for the Linotype to be worth an early start, before his retirement. Aware of the generosity of his offer, concerned about the conflict between the designs, I paused . . . and brought up Helvetica, with my reasons for thinking it critical. Jackson, champion of Trade Gothic, was silent.

Several weeks later he stopped me in the corridor, and told me that German drawings for the Helvetica series were on their way from Frankfurt. So began the first Mergenthaler face to be cut in the US directly from European drawings that had been made to European standards, in many small respects different from ours. The series was prepared with no design change, successfully adapting Didot sizes to US alignment, the first step toward a common standard to be shared by the loose confederation of Linotype companies, the foundation of the tenfold expansion of the library that was to follow.

MIKE PARKER

abcdefghijklmnopqrstuvwxyz
ABCDEFGHIJKLMNOPQRSTUVWXYZ
1234567890 .,:;''«»ß&!?

abcdefghijklmnopqrstuvwxyz
ABCDEFGHIJKLMNOPQRSTUVWXYZ
1234567890 .,:;''«»ß&!?

abcdefghijklmnopqrstuvwxyz
ABCDEFGHIJKLMNOPQRSTUVWXYZ
1234567890 .,:;''«»ß&!?

Helvetica

I've been connected with the production and release of a number of typefaces. One stands out with a satisfying 'rightness', not only in the meeting of design, place, and time, but in the warmth and generosity of those involved in the development, characteristics not always to be found in such a competitive industry.

I had joined Mergenthaler as Jackson Burke's assistant in June,1959, a time when development of new Mergenthaler designs was all but impossible. US newspapers were eliminating keying for all but local news by installing drives to operate Linotypes directly from tape. It was punched out on the spot by teletypesetter machines driven by wire service transmission. All news text characters had to be repeatedly redesigned and remanufactured to fit on rigid TTS brass widths in a series of evolving standards. A new font was required for each size of each face for each column width at each change of the standard. The drawing office and matrix factory were tied up for twenty years preparing many hundreds of TTS versions of new text designs for the industry that paid the freight.

Jackson had guarded one small corner of capacity and used it to produce our one large series for trade typesetters. Trade Gothic is a sans serif in four widths, three weights, and ten sizes, a refined and expanded linecaster version of Morris Fuller Benton's great 1908/9 series, Lightline and News Gothic. Jackson and the company saw it as an 'American' answer to the 'European' sans serifs, headed by Univers.

I worried. The European faces clearly grew out of a 20th century preoccupation with the power of figure/ground relationships, starting at the Bauhaus, developing as the central design canon in Switzerland. A student of Josef Albers and Armin Hoffmann, I saw that conscious design of sans serif white shapes to contain and guide the blacks gave these new designs a firmness, a locked in rightness, a power lacking in any of the older designs, American or European. Tastemakers were adopting Swiss designs; an international movement was gaining momentum.

The large Univers series was the market favorite, but inspection revealed difficulties for our equipment. The uniformly steep slope of italics promised duplexing disasters (later to be born out in the Matrotype series). Univers achieved uniform design across the series by applying all design limitations required by peripheral widths and weights to the core, restraining design of the central versions. Linotype mechanical limitations forbade uniformity; in our markets peripheral designs were little used. At Mergenthaler the central handle their old data of Helvetica with ATM. They wanted a clean start. In 1992, we made our URW TypeWorks product (500 masters + Inline, Outline, Relief, Shadow and Round). Now, one can have Nimbus Sans as a 'sixpack'.

In 1993, Stefan Rögener (a typograph living in Hamburg) made statistics on the use of typefaces in the advertising branch. He came out with: 'By more than 90%, the creatives use Helvetica, Futura, Garamond, and Baskerville. They are stupid. Give me a pistol.' He is still alive. But Max Miedinger died in the late seventies, poor and without glory. I can't forget Helvetica.

PETER KAROW

abcdefghijklmnopqrstuvwxyz
ABCDEFGHIJKLMNOPQRSTUVWXYZ
1234567890 .,:;'"«»ß&!?

Although I have memories of Hermann Zapf at Rudolf Hell's factory in Kiel showing us drawings of letters transferred to graph paper, and Al Friedman's great accomplishments making outlines (virtually automatically) in Skokie, and the spectacular results achieved at MGD in the early days, it is Peter Karow who properly wears the mantle of the father of the digital outline in Typography. Whatever people, particularly competitors, may have said about Ikarus it was the first system to be offered for general use and it became the only game in town, gradually evolving as the output devices for generating type became more sophisticated.

Behind it, since its inception, has been Peter Karow, usually with a little frown on his brow as he tries to explain to somebody in an unfamiliar language what he could so much more easily explain in German.

Helvetica

I started the IKARUS program late 1972. In February 1973 we had completed the digitizing and plotting parts, so we could produce the first typefaces. My first customer was Walter Florenz Brendel from Dusseldorf. He had prepared the master characters for digitizing in a large size. As we do it today: 6 inches for bodysize.

It was the typeface Olympia. I asked him whether he drew the characters himself: 'No, my designer did it.' They were inked and black/white. Later we used just pencil drawn contours. Then he added after severe questioning: 'Yes, the typeface is very close to Helvetica of the Stempel AG.' (formerly part of today's Linotype-Hell AG)

In 1976, I met with Max Miedinger. He said: 'I am the designer of the famous Helvetica. I did it in 1957. Now, Stempel earns lots of money with it, but I am out of the game. I feel cheated.'

In 1977, we digitized the Helvetica originals with IKARUS from large friskettes (rubylith letter cards at about 11 inches for bodysize). We got that service contract from the Stempel AG in Frankfurt.

In 1978, we digitized Holsatia, a Helvetica-clone made by the Hell company.

In 1980 we digitized the typeface SANS for IBM. They never used it.

In 1981, we helped the Typoart company in the DDR to digitize their Maxima, another clone of Helvetica. I guess this was the best data we ever made. One font (800 char.) included also Greek and Cyrillic and lots of accented characters.

In 1982, we digitized the Akzidenz Grotesk Buch for the Berthold company; I view it as another clone of Helvetica as did René Kerfante, manager of the Stempel AG.

In 1983, Hermann Zapf started the design of our typeface URW Grotesk because a very big publishing company (Axel Springer) wanted to have a sans serif alternative typeface.

In 1985, we did our Nimbus Sans typeface, a merger out of Helvetica, AG Buch, Holsatia and others. We tried to avoid some mistakes with the old Helvetica.

In 1986/87 the Stempel AG produced the Neue (New) Helvetica. They cloned themselves, but called it a new and innovative design.

In 1987, we digitized the Arial typeface for Monotype, another clone. This time, René Kerfante being manager at Monotype convinced me that Arial is very different from Helvetica.

In 1990, we delivered new data of Helvetica to Adobe because they could not

abcdefghijklmnopqrstuvwxyz
ABCDEFGHIJKLMNOPQRSTUVWXYZ
1234567890 1234567890 .,:;"«»ß&!?

abcdefghijklmnopqrstuvwxyz
ABCDEFGHIJKLMNOPQRSTUVWXYZ
1234567890 1234567890 .,:;"«»ß&!?

Lawrence Wallis has an insatiable appetite for new technological complexities
which beset the printing and typesetting industries. He has worked with the
Monotype Corporation and with Addressograph Multigraph, but his major
contribution to them and to us must have been in the trade press in which he
describes, explains and forecasts whatever he considers to be significant. He has
also compiled reference books on terms and facts (glossaries & chronologies). He
has recently completed a study of a vain and now rather over-looked printer.
Lawrence on the other hand is modest but immensely energetic and well-informed,
and surprisingly upbeat.
J D

Granjon

My experience has been that favoured or preferred typefaces change over time in accordance with current work preoccupations or with a developing awareness of virtues in a given design; whereas disfavoured typefaces remain eternally stigmatised.

Over the past year or longer, I have been researching a book on George W Jones (1860-1942), the distinguished London printer and adviser to the Linotype Company in Britain from 1921 until retirement in 1938. His activities were many and varied, but arguably the summit of his achievement was directing development of Granjon Old Face which first appeared in *The Linotype Record* of January 1925.

In recent months, I have become very attached to Granjon and have come to appreciate its classic dignity and helpful legibility. Much of that gracefulness stems from sensitive typographical engineering that would have been the responsibility of Harry Smith at the Altrincham factory. For example, the original non-kerning f (obligatory with linecasting) was effectively accomplished. Additionally the production of more than a score of ligatures enhanced the fluency of the design, though would have interrupted productivity of the machine compositor.

Sadly Granjon has not translated with complete satisfaction to the new technology. It began in hot-metal as a delicate and light face and those characteristics tend to be exaggerated with the split ink film of offset printing and with the thinning effects of the photomechanical processes.

Naming typefaces has traditionally been undertaken with careless abandon. Ironically Granjon is a true derivative Garamond unlike some other typefaces of that name. Beatrice Warde, through her alter ego Paul Beaujon, described the design 'as immeasurably the best of modern revivals of this letter'.

LAWRENCE WALLIS

abcdefghijklmnopqrstuvwxyz
ABCDEFGHIJKLMNOPQRSTUVWXYZ
1234567890 .,:;''«»ß&!?

abcdefghijklmnopqrstuvwxyz
ABCDEFGHIJKLMNOPQRSTUVWXYZ
1234567890 .,:;''«»ß&!?

*Don Hase can't have been more than sixteen or so when he was first thrown into
the world of typesetting, and before long he was lucky enough to come into the
orbit of the great Allan Friedman. Al in turn was busy building the capital base
that finally launched Alphatype. He designed, assembled and marketed the first
large selling headline photosetter, the Filmotype.*

*Don has probably been responsible for making more film fonts than anybody before
or after him. Even in the early sixties he had made hundreds at a time when most
people didn't even know what a film font was.*

*By now, when he has moved on to other activities nearer the 'leading edge' than
boring old type, nobody would be able to make a count.*

Goudy Oldstyle

Frederic W Goudy produced around 123 type designs before he expired.
Surely he deserves to have at least one face among the best remembered faces.
But how could he have made so many faces by himself? If so, I wonder if his
wife Bertha didn't help him? He would never get away with that today.
Bertha would be out on her own, that's for sure.
Not withstanding high marks for stick-to-it-ive-ness Goudy's Old Style is a
beautiful face, has a character of its own and is easy to read. It's a lovely face
to have around the house.
I think Goudy would never have made it in today's world. He was, you might
say, a fuss-budget about his designs, refusing to let the type founder make
even small changes. Can you imagine him trying to keep his design untouched
today? He'd be in an institution, there's no doubt.

DON HASE

abcdefghijklmnopqrstuvwxyz
ABCDEFGHIJKLMNOPQRSTUVWXYZ
1234567890 .,:;"«»ß&!?

abcdefghijklmnopqrstuvwxyz
ABCDEFGHIJKLMNOPQRSTUVWXYZ
1234567890 .,:;"«»ß&!?

Some designers seem to successfully hoe their row attended by the same loyal
clients as one decade follows another, impervious to the fluctuations of the
economy and the various fiscal disasters brought upon us by ambitious politicians.
Their knowledge is considerable and many of them therefore teach on a part time
basis and bring to their students a strong sense of quality, and the consequent
ability to distinguish between what is ephemeral and what must endure. Leo
Maggs is such a one.

Gill Sans

As every student of typography knows, the Roman alphabet, typified by the Trajan Column inscription in Rome (c. AD114), is the foundation of all Western alphabets. When many nineteenth-century type founders eschewed classic Roman proportions in favour of alphabets whose capitals were of equal width, such as Thorowgood's sans serif designs of 1832, they rightly classified them 'Grotesques'.

Edward Johnston returned to the traditional Roman form when, in 1916, he produced his famous sans serif alphabet, which later became the exclusive lettering style of London Transport. Other sans faces, such as Koch's Cable and Renner's Futura, became available by the late nineteen-twenties; but it was Eric Gill who, in 1928, refined the sans serif into something near perfection, with Gill Sans.

Then along came the new technology of photo-typesetting. This gave us the capability to reproduce a full range of type sizes from a common original – often with disastrous results. Univers, designed by Frutiger in 1957 for the French type foundry Deberny & Peignot, boasted of being the first alphabet specifically designed as 'one image for all sizes'. For this alone I grudgingly acknowledge its place in the history books. Univers reverts to the ugly uniformity of the Grotesques while Gill's Roman proportions are so much more elegant, and possessed of that essential quality Edward Johnston referred to as 'readableness'.

Block letters, lacking thick and thin strokes, really do need those variations of proportion which endow each letter with its recognizable form and character. Without them they become camouflaged by a word, and the words become camouflaged by the paragraph. Thus, not only is the elegance and beauty of the printed page dulled, but the whole process and pleasure of reading is impaired.

Down with Univers! Long live Gill Sans!

LEO MAGGS

abcdefghijklmnopqrstuvwxyz
ABCDEFGHIJKLMNOPQRSTUVWXYZ
1234567890 .,:;''«»ß&!?

abcdefghijklmnopqrstuvwxyz
ABCDEFGHIJKLMNOPQRSTUVWXYZ
1234567890 .,:;''«»ß&!?

It is undeniably with love that Romek's many students remember him, but to me
he is immovably linked to Nicholson's London Guide, that masterpiece of
compression that few of the Londoners who knew of it ever did without. If design is
about getting information to the user in the easiest way possible I know of no other
book during my reading life that did it so well. Every tool, from colour to type style
to layout, was impeccably turned to accomplish a task. I wish I had such a piece of
design to be remembered for.

Garamond

Type is like a garden full of beautiful flowers, to pick one that is best remembered is a difficult choice to make.

To have a certitude of preference for the particular is venturesome. To have an absolute certitude is brave. I prefer type which has anonymity, in which the design is not obvious or overstated, a type which is somewhat self effacing. This preference covers about all the best classical and modern typefaces and precludes me from being either venturesome or brave.

Under a cloak of classical respectability there is something incongruous about Garamond the typeface. The name is historically inaccurate yet the mistake was never corrected and the unfortunate Jean Jannon shares the fate of Christopher Columbus. As a design Garamond is irregular and even somewhat inconsistent, yet irregularity doesn't detract from the overall harmony of the type. It rather heightens the humanist facet of the design. The typeface has been modified, not always successfully, to accommodate changes in print technology, yet retained the character as if it is still 'cut by hand'.

Garamond has been in continuous use since the 17th century. In the middle of the 1950s, when I was a student at the Royal College of Art I came across the Swiss magazine *TM (Typographische Monatsblatte)*, a Swiss print review. I was attracted by the design of the magazine and the typography. The typography was 20th century Swiss, the type was Garamond.

ROMEK MARBER

abcdefghijklmnopqrstuvwxyz
ABCDEFGHIJKLMNOPQRSTUVWXYZ
1234567890 .,:;''«»ß&!?

abcdefghijklmnopqrstuvwxyz
ABCDEFGHIJKLMNOPQRSTUVWXYZ
1234567890 .,:;''«»ß&!?

One of the adages learned by graphic design students in their foundation course is 'The least said about John Miles the better.' But lost in the mists of time is the origin of the saying. Some people think that it is because it is unwise to adopt a rôle model you cannot hope to emulate.
I can now reveal that to be able to concentrate on doing good work when you are inexorably and irrevocably tied by an umbilical cord to a large hole in the ground in Suffolk is something that only John Miles can manage. Here, in relative safety at weekends, he can grow vegetables and paint without having to duck every time the low flying aircraft that buzz Snape and the whole Aldeburgh area pass overhead.

Gladdened by Galliard

Galliard is great. I could go on about the vigour of the drawing; its versatility and the pleasure of using something well made, but its real interest lies in its being made for the times we live in and the tools we use.

When the world has stopped panting after new faces and the last of the font manufacturers is complaining that they can't make a living it is the types that started life in digital form that will survive. Then abideth Charter, Swift and Galliard; these three; but the greatest of these is Galliard.

JOHN MILES

abcdefghijklmnopqrstuvwxyz
ABCDEFGHIJKLMNOPQRSTUVWXYZ
1234567890 .,:;''«»ß&!?

abcdefghijklmnopqrstuvwxyz
ABCDEFGHIJKLMNOPQRSTUVWXYZ
1234567890 .,:; ''«»ß& !?

Peter Guy has found time to practice as well as teach book design. He taught at
Oxford, and designed some innovative books in London for the Folio Society. His
panache is more noticeable in the size and style of his bow ties, but he invigorates
the meetings of the several societies and clubs to which he belongs.
J D

My Ehrhardt's Delight

An aphorism of Allen Hutt's was that the world in general – and the world of printing in particular – suffers from a panacea complex. Every new invention is hailed as the solution to all ills until such time as it is discovered that for each problem solved a dozen new ones have emerged.

Nothing demonstrated the truth of this better than the arrival of photosetting which, in the '60s, some of us were gullible enough to believe was a step forward. Even manufacturers' hype could not conceal the awful truth for long: noble, hot metal typefaces had become insipid – or worse.

It seemed to me that Ehrhardt was not only a very fine face but also almost indestructible. For something like a decade I struggled to find an alternative I could confidently use for the books I produced but almost always fell back on Ehrhardt. Nowadays I turn to great Galliard more often than not.

But recently I have returned to Ehrhardt and found it still elegant, adaptable and resilient to insensitive design and ham-fisted production.

Why was I unfaithful? Ehrhardt, I love you still.

PETER GUY

ABCDEFGHIJKLMNOPQRSTUVWXYZ
abcddefgghijklmnopqrstuvwxyz
1234567890

ABCDEFGHIJKLMNOPQRSTUVWXYZ
abcddefgghijklmnopqrstuvwxyz
1234567890

Hermann is easily the best known of contemporary type designers. His long association with the Stempel foundry must have made significant differences to how large a suitcase was needed to carry money to the bank of the parent company, Linotype AG. Palatino, Optima and Melior have all been best sellers, and probably all share two other unique distinctions. They all appeared, in turn, as the typeface most used on the letterhead of a great many leading design groups. And, except for Helvetica, they may be the most often copied faces of modern times. In the best known examples the imitation is deliberate. Most foundries, hampered in the sales of hardware because they couldn't license these faces, came out with similar – but often mechanical looking – copies. But another aspect has been that these three and also Aldus are each echoed again and again in the typefaces designed at art schools all over the world. More than once I have listened to a young designer explain the philosophy behind his new design, sometimes in Hermann's hearing, entirely unaware that, perhaps subliminally, what he has made has already been better made with one of these four faces.

Delphin

Ask a father which of several daughters he likes best, and any answer will get him into trouble. Of course he will have a special fondness for the prettiest. Type designers are like fathers to the faces they have designed, and we all know that other fathers also have pretty daughters.
I fell in love with George Trump's Delphin type when I first saw it in 1953. Or should I say her? This was an absolutely new idea in metal type at that time. It ignored the bad German standard alignment and it was courageous in its unusual proportions. In fact, every letter was an outstanding design.

HERMANN ZAPF

ABCDEGHJKMNOPQRSTUVWX

abcdefghijklmnopqrstuw

abcdefghjklmnopqrstuvwxy

ABDEGHJKLMNQRSTU

There is little in the world of printing and typesetting, in the whole business of
graphic arts in the last fifty years or more, that has not been touched by the
influence of John Dreyfus. A founder member of ATypI and its second President,
his work as the typographic adviser to Monotype, his long standing relationship
with the Pierpont Morgan Library and many other American institutions, his
numerous books, his willingness and ability to correct all our prose, each of these
occupations is almost a career in itself, and many of them have been recognised as
such. At one time or another he has received nearly every award in the business.
But here for the first time you learn that he was the model for Dorian Gray, and
his ageless appearance is matched by a portrait in his flat of such unbelievable
antiquity that even Methuselah is said to be put out by its existence.

Dante (G Mardersteig)

Opinions on Mardersteig's Dante
Range from the pro to the anti
To some it's Inferno
But to me, Paradiso –
Undeniably pure elegante

JOHN DREYFUS

de gloed van de kristalzusters was feller in hun herinnering.
nacht hielden zij de wacht bij het kamp van de zusters. Eer
nevrouw opstond van haar bed van rode kangoeroehuiden, s
de berai-berai naar de slapende meisjes toe en legden geba
koeken naast hun hoofden.
De berai-berai bleven de kristalzusters volgen als schaduw
als de nacht de dag. En op zeker ogenblik kregen ze een bej
man in zicht, die bezig was honingraten te verzamelen. De a
draaide het hoofd om en keek hen aan. Terwijl de berai-bere

Some years back R K Joshi arranged a seminar at Powai. The theme was scripts, and this drew experts from all over India, and experts from Europe, and a few spare bodies like the editor. Karina Meister was there and spent happy days out under the sun-drenched trees showing people all about Western scripts. During the progress of the seminar the students at IIT were busy taking slides. They took pictures of everything and everyone. Even if the subject didn't move they took pictures.
On the last morning they showed the result as a glorious audio visual on three screens. It was no surprise to the rest of us that the kind face that appeared on slide after slide after slide was that of the much beloved Karina Meister.

Chicago

One of my students made a small book, containing an Australian Aboriginal story named the *The Maya Maji*. She added wonderful lino-cuts (happily not what one usually calls illustration!) and for the typography I asked her to come up with a choice of 10 faces of which she thought might express the feeling of the story and graphically go well with her lino-cuts. She was to choose faces, whether she thought them available for her or not.
She made good choices of well-spaced – even color faces and had already put the text into the Mac. This she had done with Chicago and that graphic appearance she liked for her story but she did not dare to make it one of her choices. I saw it: yes, some letter combinations are not well spaced, some characters are lighter than others and the resolution is awfully coarse and yet, for this specific situation, on a kind of paper I would not easily choose for other purposes, it just is IT!! Even enlarged and electronically extremely elongated on the title page it is great, though in this case editing might have made it more refined – or too refined!!

KARINA MEISTER

abcdefghijklmnopqrstuvwxyz
ABCDEFGHIJKLMNOPQRSTUVWXYZ
1234567890 1234567890 .,:;"«»ß&!?

abcdefghijklmnopqrstuvwxyz
ABCDEFGHIJKLMNOPQRSTUVWXYZ
1234567890 1234567890 .,:;"«»ß&!?

If you speak to Ronald today it would be difficult to believe that this is the same
man who started his career in New York at the time of the early FDR. For he still
sounds as he did more than thirty years ago. A Cambridge graduate, equally at
home – though he would deny it – in Latin and Greek, he set up the US office of
the Cambridge University Press and ran it with a clear-headed efficiency and a
kindly hand so light on the reins that many people were scarcely aware of how
firmly they were held. He built this office into the Press's best outlet, and managed
also to become the University's highest paid employee.
I remember with pleasure, during a meeting at the Oxford University Press to
decide on where to print the New English Bible and how many to have for the first
impression, that the discussion and argument had wavered between 35,000 and as
much as 70,000. Uncharacteristically I held my tongue, until finally I was asked
as the sole Cambridge representative, 'What does Cambridge think?'
'Ronald Mansbridge says 600,000' I was able to reply. 'We think that may last
for six weeks, by which time we will know what the second impression should be.'
And that was what we did and that is exactly what happened.

Centaur

For a list of Types Best Remembered I nominate Centaur. I must confess that my choice is influenced, in part at least, by my life-long devotion to its designer.

I first met Bruce Rogers in 1930; great heavens, that's sixty-three years ago. I was captured at once by his modest kindness to a greenhorn. As my wife, Georgia, wrote in her monograph, Bruce Rogers, American Typographer, 'His voice was soft, his manner gentle and courteous. He liked young people.'

When we moved to Connecticut in the 1940's, not far from New Fairfield, we frequently drove over to see him at October House, often with colleagues from Cambridge, Billy Kingsford, John Dreyfus or Stanley Morison. On one such occasion BR gave Morison a sheet he had printed, with a punning parody of the opening verses of Genesis; I remember his reference to John Johnson and his 'firm o' men'. Morison accepted it without comment, but later in the car crumpled it up and threw it on the floor in disgust at what he called BR's 'triviality'. I unobtrusively rescued that crumpled paper and treasured it for years as a symbol of the different attitudes of two great men.

BR used to maintain that he did not design Centaur, but just adapted it from Jenson's original. This was over modest; virtually all types must inescapably owe something to previous models. In reviewing the type for *The Fleuron*, Morison wrote of its 'unique grace' and 'the farther Mr Rogers draws away from Jenson, the nearer he draws to our ideal face.'

When I first saw Centaur in 1930, I probably admired the 'elegance' of the sloping cross-bar of the lower-case e. I had not yet learned the lesson Morison wrote in that same issue of *The Fleuron*, 'If my friends think that the tail of my lower-case r or the lip of my lower-case e is rather jolly, you may know that the fount would have been better had neither been made.' The same comment may apply to the original design (later modified) of the lower-case y, of which T E Lawrence exclaimed, 'What a splendid y!'

But that is a tiny carp, and perhaps invalid. Centaur stands without question as a noble and graceful face, beautiful without obtruding its beauty. It was used with success in two of the most magnificent books printed in my life-time, one from Oxford, the other from Cambridge, the Lectern Bible and Morison's *Fra Luca de Pacioli*.

RONALD MANSBRIDGE

abcdefghijklmnopqrstuvwxyz
ABCDEFGHIJKLMNOPQRSTUVWXYZ
1234567890 1234567890 .,:;"«»ß&!?

Don Hase can't have been more than sixteen or so when he was first thrown into the world of typesetting, and before long he was lucky enough to come into the orbit of the great Allan Friedman. Al in turn was busy building the capital base that finally launched Alphatype. He designed, assembled and marketed the first large selling headline photosetter, the Filmotype.

Don has probably been responsible for making more film fonts than anybody before or after him. Even in the early sixties he had made hundreds at a time when most people didn't even know what a film font was.

By now, when he has moved on to other activities nearer the 'leading edge' than boring old type, nobody would be able to make a count.

Centaur

If a new world order should dictate the elimination of all but one typeface, I would be pleased if it were Centaur. It is a typeface with character and interest that is also very readable. It was, I believe, the second of the two typefaces designed by Bruce Rogers. For what ever reason, Rogers designed no more type after the release of Centaur in 1914.

For the record, I do not hold Arrighi, a face designed by Frederic Warde and selected by Rogers to be used as an italic companion with Centaur, to be at the same level. Arrighi is often listed in type books as Centaur Italic.

There is only one Centaur, no light, no medium, no bold or extrabold and no italics. Just Centaur, nothing else. Perhaps that is one of the reasons it should be remembered.

DON HASE

ABCDEGHJKMNQRSTU

Those who have known Dennis over the more than thirty years that he has been making silk purses of what have often been the sow's ears of numerous periodicals are perhaps the only ones who know how much he has influenced the way magazines look in Britain today. It is also astonishing to many of us how he ever manages to get these jobs done when he can easily spend a day considering the best way to assemble the letters that he needs to make three words. It is not astonishing, though, that he was elected a Royal Designer for Industry.

Caslon

Caslon in its original form – Stephenson Blake, Monotype, Haas. Only available in letterpress – if you can find it and can afford it. The closest Caslon film set is ATF's 540 Acceptable, but in film anyway doesn't have the sparkle of the original. All other versions, and there are quite a few, are terrible. All an insult to a beautiful typeface. Access to metal setting from founder's founts is a rare privilege. The numerals alone are a minor work of art.

DENNIS BAILEY

ABCDEFGHIJKLMNOPQRSTUVWXYZ
abcdefghijklmnopqrstuvwxyzfffifffiffl &

ABCDEFGHIJKLMNOPQRSTUVWXYZ
abcdefghijklmnopqrstuvwxyzæœ fifffffifflÆSt 1 2

We first learned to love Berlow when he was at Bitstream, when we could rely on him for ironic comments on whatever show or seminar we happened to be at. It became harder to love him as his career progressed and Font Bureau was started and shouldered its way into what is known as the 'leading edge' of font technology, and it became clear that he was getting to know more than the rest of us. Perhaps the reason we are still delighted to eat with him is that he hasn't yet got round to rubbing our noses in it.

Californian

Goudy's design for the University of California, what we call Californian, is well worth remembering. Not just because it was designed by an American in a style of typography that is as American as jazz. Not just because the designer liked to drive fast and, according to a typographer who knew him well, chase skirts faster than he drove. And not just because the face itself is so strangely primitive in its forms. Surely all of these things are true and important to me when considering the merits of a type design.

But it is the organic nature of the face, the way it seems to spring out of the earth and form spaces of such organic elegance. And yet, when the letters are placed together to form words, which of course is the sole purpose of the letters, all of the quirky organic forms of the letters join together and make typography that is even more powerful in form than the letters themselves. In other words, the words are more than the sum of the letters!

DAVID BERLOW

abcdefghijklmnopqrstuvwxyz
ABCDEFGHIJKLMNOPQRSTUVWXYZ
1234567890 .,:;''«»ß&!?

abcdefghijklmnopqrstuvwxyz
ABCDEFGHIJKLMNOPQRSTUVWXYZ
1234567890 .,:;''«»ß&!?

Walter Partridge, a perky compositor from the North of England made such a
success of his career that he was lured away from his own firm to become a labour
relations expert and manager in the Pearson group, with arduous duties at the
Financial Times. Required to negotiate as hard as he could, but never to miss an
issue, he wisely retired, and now in his early eighties prints on his own press in a
fourteenth century chapel in his house in the Close of Salisbury Cathedral. With a
Latin twist on his name, his books carry the imprint of the Perdrix Press.
He is still perky.
J D

Bembo

About typefaces. I find this a pretty boring subject, I keep coming across people who are aspiring to publish desktop books, and they boast about the 140 faces they have on their Amstrad – or what have you.

I tell them to piss off and learn a bit about leading and letter fit and word spacing before they start pontificating about poached faces.

When I returned from the FT and Westminster Press, I was given huge founts of Bembo from 10 of 11 to 48 point. Sorry, to 36 point, the 48 and 72 are Fuys Baskerville.

The Bembo, even Monotype Bembo, never mind Mardasteig's variant, is so functional for poetry and all manner of works of anything akin to a literary nature, so elegant, so economical, so erotically beautiful, that I have printed 20 titles with it – on my Arab Platen (all sold out) without ever, ever, thinking about another typeface, except a single fount of Wolpe's Albertus for the odd little line as a wrapper or binding.

I don't hate the other queer sans serifs, I just don't need them in my very limited repertoire. For example, I have just advised an editor to accept an Amstrad sans, not unlike Helvetica against a lousy Times, for a recipe book to raise funds for the Cathedral Girls Choir – the first ever, and very good too. The roman on offer was weedy and spindly – the sans carried a bit more colour, was tightly word-spaced, unjustified in small 4/5 line recipe paragraphs, and it worked well.

Horses for courses.

But never for continuous text.

Teach them close word spacing and discrete leading, give at most two decent romans and one sans and you will end up with good legibility, good communication – as they say – with little interference between author and reader.

WALTER PARTRIDGE

ABCDEFGHIJKLMNOPQRSTUVWXYZ
1234567890 .,:;"«»ss&!?

abcdefghijklmnopqrstuvwxyz
ABCDEFGHIJKLMNOPQRSTUVWXYZ
1234567890 .,:;"«»

abcdefghijklmnopqrstuvwxyz
ABCDEFGHIJKLMNOPQRSTUVWXYZ
1234567890 .,:;"«»

*Towards the beginning of Hamlet we hear about 'customary suits of solemn black'.
Hamlet was a Dane. It seems that the dress code moved West into Iceland, the
original home of the person we all know of as Briem, and only Briem. It is possible
that his mother has seen him in other colours. But since he began his peripatetic
existence, moving between the United States and Europe to escape the pollen that
chases him from season to season, none of us have seen him in anything but black.
It has its advantages. It limits the amount of decision-making needed during the
daily task of dressing. It doesn't show soup as clearly as a Garrick Club tie. But it
seems likely that when the dust has settled on all of us, and none of us can call on
him to explain why we are unable to get what we wanted on our Macintosh, he
will be best remembered for what he has achieved in the teaching of handwriting.*

Bell Centennial

In 1974, American Telephone & Telegraph commissioned the design of Bell Centennial for their phone books. For clarity in the worst of circumstances, nothing can touch it.

It was created to solve a problem. Uneven printing and rough paper are a punishment on lettershapes. Delicate lines get wiped out. Ink fills nooks and crannies. Bell Centennial allows for this in the design. It looks just right after the presses have done their worst. I like it for two reasons. I admire a solution by logic and common sense, and I admire grace. Plenty of designs compensate for distortion. Matthew Carter created a bulletproof rhinoceros that could dance Swan Lake.

The type was released in 1978, fulfilling great expectations of legible phone books. More text could also go on each page than before. Less paper was needed, and AT&T saved a fortune. Careful use of paper is more important now than ever it was. Printing costs have got no better. In addition, people have taken to worrying about trees. Using less paper is far better than recycling it. When that stuff eventually goes into landfills, it has enough glue and preservatives to outlast plutonium. And somewhere there are forests still standing, with the assortment of badgers and possums that call them home, because of Bell Centennial. The London telephone directories have used it since 1989, slightly modified, to much environmental praise.

In a world of clamor and gimmicks, quality easily passes unnoticed. This type design remains a yardstick that other attempts at legibility are measured against. Getting to know it is a great pleasure.

GUNNLAUGUR S E BRIEM

abcdefghijklmnopqrstuvwxyz
ABCDEFGHIJKLMNOPQRSTUV
WXYZ 1234567890 .,:;"«»ß&!?

abcdefghijklmnopqrstuvwxyz
ABCDEFGHIJKLMNOPQRSTUVW
XYZ 1234567890 .,:;"«»ß&!?

Presenting a little book that he and Frances Butler had made at the Poltroon
Press in San Francisco, Alastair Johnston once addressed a dinner at Queens
College Cambridge. In his talk we learned, via Mark Twain, that in Mark
Twain's early life in a newspaper office a man who could set 700 ems an hour
could put on any airs he wanted to. But he also told us that some New York
compositors, on a wager, had set 2000 ems an hour of minion for four hours at a
stretch. Minion, as you all know, was just a little over 7pt, and these men were
therefore picking up around four thousand very small pieces of type in an hour and
arranging them in a stick. That is more than one a second, and they had to be
selected in order!
It seems to me that there are more Scots out of Scotland than there are Scots in
Scotland. But it also seems to me that they are more erudite than the rest of us.

Bell

Bell type, named for an enterprising newspaperman and publisher of the Georgian era, was cut by an engraver named Richard Austin in 1787. The transitional period, after Baskerville, but before the new wave characterised by Bodoni washed away subtlety in a tide of stark bravado and hairline serifs, was a couple of short decades, during which the finest types ever cut were engraved in France and England.

Less spindly and a little squarer than Baskerville, and tighter fit, Bell's type was apparently modelled on those of François Ambroise Didot of 1781, with sharp modelling, a vertical stress, and fine tapering bracketed serifs. To my eye the Paragon letters cut by Austin are the most beautiful ever created: the caps are robust, the contorted elements like the lower case a and g"are perfectly articulated. The matching cursive italic (again following Baskerville) is a masterpiece of understatement, though there is exuberance in the swash caps, T, N, J, Y, & Q. The cap R has a characteristically British arched leg which is echoed in upper and lower case k. The cap J sits on the baseline. Austin also cut lining figures, to the height of small capitals, so for the first time figures were well integrated into the font.

The vertical stress and sharper modelling indicated the future direction for type, following the lead of Firmin Didot, whose refined modern types of 1795 have flat unbracketed serifs. Austin was followed in transitional style by William Martin (who cut Bulmer's types), Joseph Fry, and Binny & Ronaldson in Philadelphia, but the style was short-lived. Soon the modern swamped type design. Austin himself cut the modern types of William Miller that became the basis of Scotch Roman. The history of the rediscovery of Bell in America by Bruce Rogers and D B Updike, and its revival in England by Stanley Morison, is well known. Bell was recast from the original matrices and re-issued by Monotype in 1931. The latest digital version from Monotype, however, is not up to par, lacks many characters, and is a pale reminder of the glory of the real thing.

ALASTAIR JOHNSTON

abcdefghijklmnopqrstuvwxyz

ABCDEFGHIJKLMNOPQRSTUVWXYZ

1234567890 .,:;"«»ß&!?

abcdefghijklmnopqrstuvwxyz

ABCDEFGHIJKLMNOPQRSTUVWXYZ

1234567890 .,:;"«»ß&!?

After the 39-45 war W S Cowells was one of the companies in the forefront of offset printing. It was there that a facsimile edition of some of the King's stamp collection was printed. I can't remember how many runs there were in total. The sheet I saw being run was the 27th colour. And it was at about this time that I saw the first of John Lewis' books, a Cowells show piece, the cloth cover printed in at least four colours and the inside packed with illustrations by people like Edward Bawden, Linton Lamb and John Piper, the leading names of the day. It was only later that I discovered his beautiful books on wooden boats. It can probably be expected that anybody who had spent time on the east coast of England in those days would be bitten by the same bug, but few could have put it to such good use for the rest of us.

Baskerville

In 1946 I started work at Cowells in Ipswich. My knowledge of typography was minimal. The first day I was there I visited the Composing Room. With its ranks of type cases it had not changed since the 1850s. The Overseer, whose name was Schofield, was an elderly bulldogish figure with beetling black eyebrows. He came from Manchester. When he discovered how little I knew of his trade, he sighed and then gave me a piece of advice.

'Well, Lad' he said, 'whenever you are putting a book together, if in doubt, set it in Baskerville.'

A week or so later, during one lunch break, I called at a booksellers in Silent Street, called the College Gateway. Mr Cook, the owner, was a garrulous character but for once his talk had some relevance to my needs.

'I've got an old album I would like to show you. It is full of old printers' marks, playbills, For Sale Notices, engraved title pages and a Baskerville Specimen Sheet. I'll get it for you.'

In a few moments he returned, struggling with a huge elephant sized portfolio. He dropped it on the counter and we were enveloped in dust. The Baskerville Specimen Sheet was loose. I picked it up and looked at it carefully. It was exquisitely printed from the most precise and elegant typefaces.

'How much?' I asked.

'Two pounds.' he replied.

'What, for the Baskerville sheet?'

'No, no, for the whole album.' he replied irascibly.

On the strength of that Baskerville sheet and a Prayer Book from the same founder, I based my typographic style. It was an unfashionable choice, at a time when the classic types of the Italian and the French masters of the trade or the post-Bauhaus sans serif fashions of the Swiss typographers led the field. Over the next forty years I have remained faithful to the Birmingham typefounder, with on occasions breaking out into Ehrhardt, and on one, and one only, occasion setting a book in Univers. This was my *The Twentieth Century Book.*

JOHN LEWIS

abcdefghijklmnopqrstuvwxyz
ABCDEFGHIJKLMNOPQRSTUVWXYZ
1234567890 .,:;"«»ß&!?

abcdefghijklmnopqrstuvwxyz
ABCDEFGHIJKLMNOPQRSTUVWXYZ
1234567890 .,:;"«»ß&!?

When photoheadline setting started as a serious industry in the early sixties Bill Thomson and Ken Whelan were among the first to turn it into an art form. It was from these beginnings that spacing, and the ability to see such fine distinctions in the treatment of letters, that to the initiated the hand that composed a poster was no more anonymous than the experienced hand sending morse code is to other morse people. Bill was probably also the first person to set more than 150 words an hour, yet he may be remembered for longer as the one with so much asparagus in his garden that he could cut it, he claimed, with a scythe.

Baskerville

When Robert was kind enough to ask me to contribute a piece for *Types Best Remembered – Best Forgotten*, it cannot have occurred to him that he might be giving rise to a popular radio programme. For it was whilst I was trying to reduce a short list of favourite type faces to only one that I had a flash of inspiration and wrote immediately to the BBC outlining my ideas for 'Castaway Founts'.

The basis of Castaway Founts is that a well known printer or graphic designer has to imagine that they have been marooned on a desert island with a printing press, an unlimited supply of paper and eight typefaces. The presenter, (Sue Lawley springs to mind as someone eminently suitable), would then invite the celebrity to discuss their selections and encourage them to reminisce about their life and how events had influenced their choice of founts. The programme concludes with a natural disaster that carries away all but one of the faces, and the subject discloses which of the eight they would save and why.

So when Sue asks me which of my eight I would save, it would be Monotype Baskerville. Firstly because of a shared interest with the designer in large dogs, although, unlike Baskerville, I have not suffered from any of the behaviour problems that provoked him into having his dog put down. Secondly because I believe this typeface is ideal for most purposes. It is delightfully proportioned and therefore legible in all sizes, with a strong bold that contrasts well with the roman, unlike Bembo or Garamond where the bold is a little thin, whilst the italic is attractively flourished yet still manages to complement the roman. There is a wide range of extra sorts, with both aligning and non-aligning figures, the lack of which has spoilt many an otherwise beautiful piece of typography. Exceptionally, the design has withstood the transfer from metal to film setting without loss of character, and looks well on a wide range of papers.

I have not as yet heard from the BBC concerning my proposals for the programme, but it can't be long before I do; no producer worth his salt could turn down a script with human interest as well as a clever pun in the title.

BILL THOMSON

Dennis Bailey doesn't like Palatino, and Colin Cohen can throw everything else away if he has it. Neither is a novice to type. This is not for them the same as our growing out of the Grieg piano concerto that once seemed the greatest music ever written.

I used to feel that way about Perpetua Titling. And I grew out of it. It seemed too pretty, too obvious, to sit happily on a page. Now, perhaps, like Dennis Bailey I will come back to it again. I even suspect that the only thing stopping me is that since it has been digitised it has also been homogenised.

I have said in some other article that I can think of no thing made by man that is so widely used as type. Not shoes, not clothes, not even whisky. But I can be sure that many people will be able to point out how wrong I am. What strikes me as odd is that this stuff, this type, whose job is to be inconspicuous, to create as smooth a passage as possible between the writer and the reader, is – perhaps because of this – also a product that hardly anybody knows anything about. Perhaps it is good for us, who should know something about type, to learn that we know hardly anything. Few of us can say how we recognise it, or even why we like one face.

What we do know is that we can have hours of enjoyment from talking about it. It is proper for me to end by hoping that all these people who made time to send a contribution will enjoy the book as much as we who have been putting it all together in spare moments during a few days in October.

The reader will be well aware that each typeface has many derivatives and versions – the discerning eye of the contributor may well be glazed by the particular Type 1 version chosen for this book. The purpose of the artwork is to give an idea of the face: the quality of the reproductions in some cases falls short of the ideal. This is often the way when things have had to be retrieved from rubbish bins and other such desperate places. The production team make no apology for this, due to the intense and probably unworkable timescale set by the editor.

ROBERT NORTON

Introduction

The idea for this book came more than twenty years ago, after Allen Hutt had died. Allen was the doyen of newspaper design, and because he lived his life with enthusiasm and delight, not to mention a touch of ribaldry, he improved every gathering he attended. He was definitely a type worth remembering. But the book never got made.

Neither has the current resurrection gone as I expected. I expected small paragraphs extolling personal favourites, and larger paragraphs vilifying all the obvious whipping boys. But it hasn't happened like that. We all expected to find Souvenir among the forgotten. Souvenir is in a class by itself. We could expect people to raise objections. But Palatino?

And how is it that nobody objected to Bookman with swashes? Can there be a typeface that has less to do with what makes a typeface beautiful or functional?

What I find particularly interesting is that many other people share my view that there can be a lovely face badly made, and the badness of the making is enough to stop people using that face. Plainly it must distress Hermann Zapf to see his children abused. But I am pleased that it also disturbs Alastair Johnston to see Bell become less with each making. I agree about Bell, and Bell is not my child. Bell is nobody's child any more. But Bell still deserves protection. I have always felt the same about Centaur. Each making seems less than the one before.

Yet if we are prepared to listen to Beethoven sonatas in a lousy recording, when the recording may be also competing against car noises, because we are reminded of the original, why is it that many of us would rather not use a face at all than use a bad rendering of it? What is the difference?

We are learning that there are qualities in type design that we do not even have the vocabulary to describe. Matthew Carter points out that a great typeface is identifiable before you can even distinguish the words. But this is also true of very ugly ones. Just as we can identify those people we know well, particularly our children, by their walk or by the way they stand, so can we tell typefaces by the colour they make on the page. But it isn't only the colour. It is another quality we cannot even specify.

What you may want to think about after you have dipped in this book for a while is to what extent we can be objective about typefaces. I say categorically that Bookman with swashes is ugly.

Is it really?

This book is dedicated to

Allen Hutt,
Harold Hunter,
&
Merald Wrolstad

and to
Tim Wood

And to
all kindred spirits
wherever they may be

The contributors are named, and
John Dreyfus also furnished some
biographical spots when I looked like flagging

Typeset by all sorts of people including some at
Petr van Blokland's workshop in Antwerp

Printed and bound in Italy by
Sergio Zanchetta at
Grafica Gilcar
Via Giuba 11
20132 Milano

through the good offices of
Sebastiano Castiglioni

Thanks too to Erik Blegvad for his
Man of letters

and to
Stephen Lovell-Davis
for his Alphabet Soup pictures

and to Des Edmonds
for his unfailing generosity in moments of panic

and to James Mosley
who let us raid the St Bride library
for references

and to my three daughters
who all helped to scramble the material together
in the few hours that remained after the last entries arrived,
before the artwork had to go to Milan

Edited by Robert Norton
© 1993 Parsimony Press

ISBN 1-884606-00-8

A

COLLECTION

OF

OBSERVATIONS

ON

Types *Best Remembered*

BY

VARIOUS

PEOPLE

CHARITABLY

DISPOSED

TO AN

EXPATRIATE

EDITOR

PARSIMONY PRESS

Types *Best Remembered*